clearing
the
clutter

clearing the clutter

100 ways to energize your life

Mary Lambert

CICO BOOKS

London

First published in Great Britain by
Cico Books
32 Great Sutton Street
London EC1V 0NB
(020) 7253 7960

10 9 8 7 6 5 4

A CIP catalogue record for this book is available from the British Library

ISBN 1 903116 13 9

Designed by Roger Daniels

Illustrators
Sam Wilson (pp 5, 11, 12, 17, 20, 28, 34, 35, 41, 46,
47, 53, 56, 57, 62, 63, 71, 77, 82, 84)

Kate Simunek (pp 10, 22, 28, 32, 33, 38, 39, 45,
50, 54, 55, 60, 61, 67, 74, 75, 80, 81)

Reproduction by Alliance Graphics, Singapore

Printed and bound in Singapore by Tien Wah Press

Contents

Introduction

An accumulation of clutter in our homes is something we all suffer from, but it is whether we manage to keep it under control, or whether it starts to control us that is important. Feng shui is the ancient Chinese practice of furniture placement and energy flow in the home. Improving the flow of energy and creating good feng shui can bring about increased prosperity, better health, and increased personal success. To achieve good feng shui in the home environment, it is first essential to clear out clutter. This is a powerful process that cleanses the space, helping to bring about amazing changes in the occupants' lives. Other feng shui changes or cures can be implemented after the clear-out.

A major part of feng shui is controlling the flow of chi (energy) in the home. A feng shui consultant's aim, when she visits a client, is to manipulate and balance this energy, so that it moves positively through all the rooms. When chi enters the home and encounters obstructions, it slows down. Piles of clutter in a home create blockages that restrict the flow of chi, making it sluggish, and this has a detrimental effect on the occupants. The trouble is that once clutter starts to build up, it attracts more, and before you know it your home is a clutter nightmare. The sticky, slow energy that surrounds your junk makes you feel reluctant to progress in every area of your life, influencing you mentally, emotionally and spiritually.

MOVING ON

The main definition of clutter is things that you no longer use or love (see page 8, 16–17). The trouble with most of us is that we have a tendency to form a strong emotional attachment to our possessions. So, even when an object is no longer useful, we still keep it, convincing ourselves that one day we will use it again. It is the same with unwanted presents and strange things that we have inherited: we always associate the item with the person who gave it to us, and then we can't let it go. When we do finally manage to throw out or give such things away, the feeling is liberating. Hanging on to too many old possessions also keeps us linked to our past, and does not allow us to move on.

A NEW LIFE

The aim of *Clearing the Clutter* is to help you begin the process of clearing out, because the longer you leave it, the harder it is to start.

It explains why you are hoarding junk and how your life will change when you dispose of it, a little at a time. The major 'clutter zones' in your home are identified, along with checklists and clutter-busting ideas. When your home is junk-free, there are plenty of ideas on boosting chi, while the final chapter shows you how to use feng shui enhancements such as water features, plants and crystals.

The possessions that you keep in the kitchen need to be thought about carefully as in every other area of the home.

By streamlining your home and removing things that are no longer needed, you will create a place that nurtures and embraces you. You will find out what you really want in life, and allow space for new people and exciting opportunities to enter.

You are Your Clutter!

Clutter clearing is a powerful process that will bring startling changes in your life. Don't add crystals and other feng shui enhancements until you have tackled your clutter, because they just will not work.

In cluttered areas of your home, chi (energy) stagnates, and once this stale energy has accumulated, it will grow even more. Junk mail, abandoned craft projects, newspapers waiting for recycling – all constitute clutter. Clutter also means all those neglected items that you hide in corners, thinking you will make a decision about them later – but you never do. Avoiding a drastic clear-out can stem from a fear of the future, but once you commit to it, you will move on and change.

YOUR INNER SOUL

Your home is supposed to mirror your inner self, so mess and inactivity reflects something that is going on inside of you. The chaos will also make you feel lethargic, stultified and confused about what you want in your life. Once you have emptied out your junk hoard, you will feel physically, emotionally and spiritually liberated, and you will have opened the door to wonderful new opportunities.

What clearing out means

If your clutter is getting you down and you want to start getting rid of it, you are ready to make changes in your life to bring yourself closer to what you want. Don't underestimate the effects a clear-out can have on you. You may find it painful to get rid of possessions that you have kept for a long, long time, and feel that you cannot exist without them, even though an inner voice is telling you to let go. Once you have done this, you need to evaluate honestly what is relevant to your life now and in the future.

Think positively: saying that you feel you will be happier when the clutter is gone is not enough. Make a list of short-term and long-term goals, such as changing careers, starting a new business, having more free time for artistic pursuits, creating an area for hobbies, or embarking on a new relationship. Setting goals makes de-junking easier, because you are mentally clearing the pathway to your dreams.

You will feel much happier in yourself when you have cleared out rooms such as the bedroom and installed good storage units.

The flow of chi

According to the Chinese view of the universe, there is an invisible life force or energy, called chi, that flows through all things. Manipulating and balancing the flow of chi in the home is a major part of feng shui practice. When chi moves freely, the atmosphere is bright, charged and feels uplifting.

The chi that flows through the home needs to have a strong movement in order to have a positive and beneficial impact on all the people who live there. It enters through the front door and then meanders through the rooms in a spiralling movement (see right), finding an exit through a back door and windows.

Clutter is the biggest obstacle to a smooth flow of chi, because it creates a blockage that chi cannot easily get around. When this occurs in the porch and hallway, for example, which are considered to be the 'mouth' of the home, it prevents sufficient chi from entering. If there is mess everywhere, chi will struggle sluggishly around the house. This will in turn affect the occupants, making them feel confused or stuck in a rut. Feng shui consultants who are sensitive to energy flow may sense these stagnant areas by their stale, musty odour and a sticky feel.

Chi enters each room in the house and constantly forms spirals like wisps of smoke as it works its way from the door to the window. Chi also comes through the window and meanders towards the door.

THE ENERGY OF POSSESSIONS

When you surround yourself with articles that you love and often use, they emit a vibrant energy that encourages the normal flow of chi and helps to produce an atmosphere that makes your life feel joyful and happy. Loved possessions seem to support and nurture you through invisible connecting strands. However, if you surround yourself with unwanted junk or useless, broken items, their negative emanations will only pull you down. The longer these piles of rubbish stay around, the worse their effects will be on you. Throw away everything that has no particular meaning for you, and you will shed a heaviness that will boost you mentally, physically and spiritually.

When your home is a mess, it is difficult to find the things that you need. When your house keys have gone missing again, important letters have disappeared into the black hole that is a stack of junk mail, your mobile phone has vanished and those shoes you so want to wear are buried somewhere at the back of the wardrobe – it's time for action. This constant muddle mixes up the energy from these items and you reflect this by becoming confused and stressed, rather than being calm and in command. So, by resolving the outer mess in your home and kick-starting the flow of chi, your inner confusion will disappear and life will certainly start to improve.

If your home is full of junk, you will constantly have problems finding items that you regularly use such as your keys, mobile phone and favourite pair of shoes.

Tied to your past

One of the problems that we all have with clearing out clutter is that we form such a strong emotional attachment to our possessions. Gazing fondly at ornaments or other accessories that people have given us over the years makes us feel secure. We even hang on to mementoes that are associated with an unhappy event, because we convince ourselves that we really do love them.

WHAT SHOULD YOU KEEP?

It is perfectly acceptable to keep some possessions that remind you of happy times, provided that when you look at them, you are filled with love. But if you have too many, your energies will be linked too strongly to your past, preventing new things from entering your life. Giving away or throwing out items that you strongly identify with can prove very painful emotionally, because it is like parting with a bit of yourself or rejecting a friend's generosity. When a friend selects a gift for you, it is chosen with a certain intention, often love, and these feelings then get tied up in the vibration of the object – which is why we find it so hard to let go of it. However, the truth is that once you have relinquished some possessions, you often don't miss them at all. Also, if you give them to someone who will love them just as much as you did, you will feel good about it.

DO YOU NEED TO PRUNE YOUR POSSESSIONS?

◆ Do your possessions mainly reflect your past?

◆ Look at your home objectively and see what it reveals – do you sense fear of the future in the chaos you have created?

◆ If you gave away several objects from your living room, would it really have a negative effect on your life?

◆ Are your deep feelings about some of your possessions holding you back from a brighter, better future?

◆ Do you see hosts of memories in all your rooms, and realize no new ones are being created?

If you answer 'yes' to these questions, you definitely need to get rid of some stuff: so start pruning.

If you are finding it really hard to get rid of some items that you no longer use but which have wonderful memories, take photos of them and put them in bound books so when you throw them away you will not feel the loss so acutely.

RELEASING POSSESSIONS

It can be hard to give away or sell items inherited from deceased relatives. Even though you may never have liked a piece, it relates to that person in the form of an emotional tie, or energy, that you are reluctant to sever.

You may believe that your possessions are visible symbols of the person you are. But when there are so many that they dominate your home, you may be subconsciously building a memorial to your past life – and if you do let something go, it seems as if part of you is going as well. But once you have started this process of release, you will not look back and new energy will come flooding into your life.

Using the Pa Kua

If you are having a disastrous time in one area of your life and nothing seems to improve it, check to see if clutter is causing the problem. The Pa Kua is a basic feng shui tool. It is an octagonal figure that corresponds to the cardinal points of the compass and the four sub-directions. It contains eight ancient symbols called trigrams, which are believed to be very powerful.

The Pa Kua has six rings. The first ring shows the trigrams; the second shows the Chinese name for the trigrams; the third ring relates to the five Chinese elements – Wood, Metal and Earth have two directions, and Fire and Water have one. The fourth ring indicates the colours associated with each element; the fifth has the eight compass directions, while the sixth ring shows the life aspirations – the southeast, for example, corresponds to wealth and prosperity, while the north links to career prospects. The Pa Kua can be placed on a plan of the whole house, or a single room, to make a feng shui diagnosis. Various parts of the home represent each life aspiration, and these can be activated to improve your luck in that area.

HOW CLUTTER AFFECTS YOUR LIFE

Now go around your home to see how your clutter affects your life aspirations. If your largest pile of mess is in your wealth section, this explains why your finances have been suffering. If some is in your marriage area, it can bring problems to an existing relationship or prevent a new one; in your recognition and fame section, you can become less popular and lack enthusiasm.

Recognition and Fame
South
Red
Fire
Li

Marriage and Romantic Happiness
Southwest
Yellow
Strong Earth
K'un

Wealth and Prosperity
Southeast
Green
Small Wood
Sun

Children
West
Metallic, White, Gold
Small Metal
Tui

Family and Health
East
Green, Brown
Strong Wood
Chen

Education and Knowledge
Northeast
Beige
Small Earth
Ken

Career Prospects
North
Black, Blue
Water
K'a

Mentors and Networking
Northwest
Metallic, White, Gold
Strong Metal
Chien

DRAWING A PLAN OF YOUR HOME

You need to find out where the eight life aspirations are in your home, so that you can see if they are being negatively affected by clutter.

◆ First, buy a good-quality orienteering compass. Then, with compass in hand, stand looking out of your front door to discover the direction that your home faces, making sure that you align the north end of the needle with the north point of the compass.

◆ Draw a scale plan of your home. Find the plan's centre by drawing two diagonal lines from the corners and mark where they cross. Position the compass here.

◆ Mark the eight compass points on the plan: north, northeast, east, southeast, south, southwest, west and northwest.

◆ Place a copy of the Pa Kua over the house plan, ensuring that the compass points match the Pa Kua sections. Note down which areas of your home relate to each life aspiration and then keep for reference.

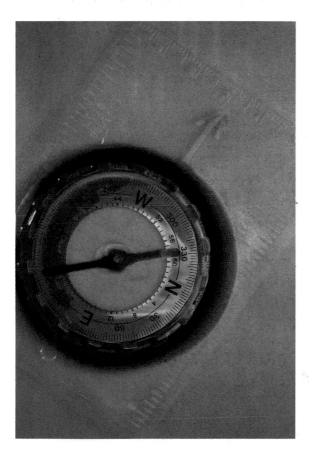

Clutter in your children's sector, for example, will inhibit your relationships with children and young people and hamper creativity; a blocked mentors and networking area shuts off support from friends and contacts, while a restricted career section will make your job seem like an endless struggle. Overflowing junk in your education sector limits your aptitude for learning and making good decisions. In your family area, clutter can cause regular conflict with family members.

Now that you know how the eight life aspiration areas of your home are afflicted, you can start by clearing out the worst area and see how fast changes can happen.

An orienteering compass is all that you need to get the basic directions of your home.

Clearing Out to Move on

There is no doubt about it – a cluttered home brings about a cluttered mind. If your household is bursting with vast amounts of clutter, chi stagnates and will not flow smoothly through each room. This can have a negative effect on you – you may feel that your life is in a rut, your confidence may plummet or you may suffer from depression or tiredness. Holding on to possessions that you are emotionally attached to can keep you linked to the past and stop you moving forward in life.

To find out if you are hoarding unnecessary junk, fill in the questionnaire opposite. Take no more than five minutes – your first answers are usually the most truthful. You can then start to work on the areas of your home that need the most attention.

Clearing out unwanted items from rooms such as the bathroom will help you to move on in your life.

ARE YOU A JUNK HOARDER?

This questionnaire will help you to assess just how much clutter has accumulated in your life. Score two points for a 'Yes', one for a 'Sometimes' and zero for a 'No'.

Yes   No   Sometimes

1 Your wardrobe is stuffed with clothes that you don't wear.

2 Odd socks and tights that have seen better days lurk in bedroom drawers.

3 You keep magazines for more than a year.

4 You have several appliances that don't work, but never get around to getting them fixed.

5 Piles of newspapers are stacked for recycling, but you never take them to the recycling centre.

6 Old suntan creams and discarded cosmetics hibernate at the back of the bathroom cabinet.

7 There is a cache of old sports gear or leisure equipment, which has been used once and then relegated to the loft, never to be seen again.

8 There is a drawer full of mysterious old keys that don't seem to open anything.

9 Piles of old, often not very good, holiday photos of people that you don't remember are now taking up cupboard space.

10 Your handbag and purse are awash with old notes, bus and train tickets, receipts from months ago and other useless trivia.

11 Old files, papers and pens that don't work have found a permanent home in your briefcase.

12 Your car is rattling with apple cores, cassette tapes that have died, and chocolate wrappers.

13 You are reluctant to invite friends to stay in your spare room because it has so much old furniture in it.

14 You have pieces of furniture that are all in need of some sort of repair.

15 Unfashionable and unloved ornaments are tucked out of sight in one of your cupboards.

16 Your garage is so full of junk that you can't get the car in it any more.

17 You have a collection of old, rusting garden equipment that you never use.

18 People keep tripping over all the boxes and other items that you store in the hall.

19 You still have theatre or music programmes from several years ago.

20 Your computer is crammed with files that you never refer to any more.

TOTAL SCORE

THE RESULTS

15–20
Your home and life are well and truly cluttered. It's time for drastic action, so work out what you really want and what you can happily chuck out. Now consider what extra storage you need for the valued possessions that have survived the cull. Look at the storage you already have and decide how new furniture will fit in, before rushing out and buying.

10–14
Clutter is building up, so get a grip on it now.

5–9
You do not have a problem with clutter yet, but do monitor yourself.

Below 5
Your home is virtually clutter-free – so try to keep it that way.

Space-clearing rituals

De-junking each room (see pages 32–79) will help stagnant chi flow freely again. However, you may need a stronger method of changing the energy to suit different circumstances.

All the events that happen in a home create energies that become imprinted into its structure. Emotional upsets and illness leave a stronger impression, and patterns that repeat themselves get deeply imprinted. So if, for example, the previous occupants of your home got divorced, there is a likelihood that the people before them did as well, and that this powerful residual energy (predecessor energy) will cause relationship problems.

To shift and cleanse lurking negative energies, so that your life is not affected detrimentally, you need to perform a space-clearing ritual.

ENERGY-BOOSTING TIPS

Use these tips as additional ways of improving your home's energy.

- Give your home a good spring-clean to lift the energy.
- Bring more energy in by opening all the doors and windows.
- Light candles to create yang, fire energy.
- Arrange some fresh flowers, removing dried flowers or any dead or dying plants.

WHICH RITUAL DO I PERFORM?

There are some quite complicated rituals that require the services of an experienced space-clearing consultant, but you can do the following more simple techniques yourself.

Smudging: Smouldering herbal smudge sticks are a popular way of cleansing the energy of a home (see page 22).

Aromatherapy oils: A few drops of essential oil are added to a mister filled with water, and sprayed around to change the energy vibration (see page 24).

Clapping: This simple technique is used to shift energy that has become stuck in a room.

Incense: The smoke from burning incense sticks is trailed around a room to change the energy levels (see page 26).

Natural salt: This traditional method of purification helps neutralize negative energies.

HOW TO BEGIN

Do not attempt space clearing if you are feeling physically or emotionally unwell, or if you are apprehensive about it for any reason. Avoid it also if you are menstruating, pregnant, or have an open cut. Clean your home well the day before, have a bath or shower before you start, and take off any jewellery.

Candles can be used as basic energizers to lift the atmosphere in a specific room.

When to space-clear

If you just want to generally clear the energies in your home, perform one of the space-clearing ceremonies detailed on the following pages. There are also particular times when creating an energy shift with these techniques will be beneficial to you and your family. Smudging and misting with essential oils are both very effective for deep cleansing. The other methods are best used in combination with these for intensive space clearing.

AFTER AN ARGUMENT

The oppressive atmosphere that lingers after a serious argument hangs like a black cloud. It can be very unsettling and, if it is not dispelled, it can adversely affect the mood of people who enter the room. Misting with essential oils of lavender, chamomile or geranium works well. To remove emotional negativity, just mist with water on its own. Water creates negative ions that flood the atmosphere, creating an

Fresh-smelling herbs, such as sweetgrass, are used in dried form in the smudging technique to space-clear. Other herbs, such as basil, lemon and lavender, are used in essential oil form and are diluted with water in a mister. The solution is sprayed around the home or room to clear the atmosphere. Lavender essential oil has the same effect as neutral chi and is therefore particularly effective for clearing bad, stuck energy.

invigorating feeling, similar to the euphoria felt by the sea. Incense, too, can shift heaviness.

AFTER ILLNESS OR DEATH

Wash the bedlinen that was used in the sickroom, and do a space-clearing ceremony on the whole house so that you refresh all the energy. Thorough cleansing is advisable after death because although it is a natural process, grief and upset linger, and sometimes the person's spirit does not move on easily.

Smudging with sweetgrass is powerful, and misting with essential oil of eucalyptus, lemon, tea tree or rosemary lifts the atmosphere.

AFTER MOVING

History can repeat itself, so it is always a good idea to space-clear a new home, because there may be residual negative energies from previous owners. Smudging with sage or rosemary is beneficial, or you can mist with essential oil of lavender, sage, pine, fir, rosemary or juniper. Use salt for extra cleansing power.

TO PROGRESS

Sometimes you are at a dead end in your life, perhaps unable to make any positive progress. Or there may be a problem that you can't resolve. But by space-clearing your home, you can change the energy and allow solutions to enter. Clapping shifts trapped energy, while misting with basil, lemon and clary sage can improve mental clarity. Smudging with cedar needles dispels a dull atmosphere.

Herb plants can help to energize a room, while herb aromas have been used by native cultures to literally 'clear the air'.

Space-clearing techniques

SMUDGING

In ancient times, smoke was used in religious ceremonies for purification, and to make a connection with the spirits of the air. Smudging is a Native American tradition, often used by well-known space-clearer Denise Linn. Bundles of tightly-bound, dried herbs are lit and allowed to smoulder. The stick is then carefully carried around a chosen area so that its smoke will cleanse any negative energies and purify the atmosphere.

A number of different herbs can be used for smudging ceremonies, but the most popular ones are sage, sweetgrass, rosemary and cedar needles. Sage was popular traditionally for its strong purification powers, while sweetgrass, with a distinctive, fresh smell similar to new-mown hay, was believed to remove negative energies.

When you are smudging, make sure that you waft the smoke all around the room, including all the corners and nooks and crannies.

Buying herbs for smudging

Prepared herbal bundles for smudging, called smudge sticks, can be bought from natural health stores and some bookstores specializing in mind, body and spirit titles. You can also make your own sticks by collecting herbs, tying the ends together with string and hanging them upside-down in a cool place to dry.

The smudging ceremony

Light your smudge stick – you may need to blow on it to get it burning – and when it is well alight, extinguish the flames, leaving the herbs smouldering. Always hold the stick over a fireproof dish to catch any sparks.

Before you begin to cleanse your home or a specific room, you should smudge yourself to clear your thoughts, emotions and aura (your body's energy field). To do this, offer up your smoking herbs to the spirits then, opening out your hands, draw the smoke gently towards your eyes and then the rest of your face and head. Slowly carry on drawing the smoke to the rest of your body and your aura, asking for cleansing of each area. This process will help to give you the energy to begin the purification of your home.

Smudging a room

Change into some casual or old clothes, wash your hands, and then, starting at the front door or the door of a specific room, walk clockwise around the room, holding the herbs and dish in one hand. With your free hand, waft the smoke along the walls and into all the corners, cupboards, bookshelves and units. If the energy in one place feels heavier, waft the smoke into it more briskly. Ask the spirit of the property to dispel negative energies and allow positive energy to flow once more. Smudging reaches

Sage and rosemary are two of the most popular herbs to use for space-clearing as they are good for removing negative energies.

deeply embedded old energy and releases it. As you finish, close the door.

Repeat the process in other rooms, if necessary. When you have finished the ritual, extinguish the stick under running water, cut off the burnt bit and put away the stick (a small stick lasts for three smudging sessions, a large one for six or seven). Repeat the smudging technique every day, for two to three days, until the energy shifts, then smudge once a week as needed. Also, bear in mind that the smudging smoke is very pungent, so you will need to open windows and doors after each session to clear the atmosphere.

As you will have also cleansed your aura, your clothes and hair will smell of smoke, so you may need to wash your clothes and take a shower after the ceremony, and thoroughly wash your hair.

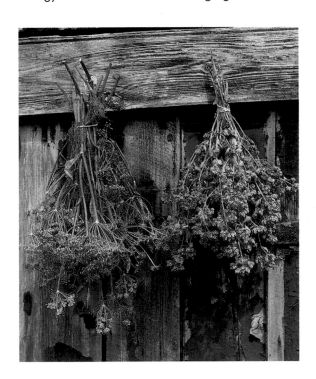

If you want to make your own smudge sticks, collect your chosen herbs, tie them with some string, and hang them upside down on a hook or nail to dry.

AROMATHERAPY

Essential oils are distilled naturally from herbs and plants. They have a wonderful smell and retain the life force, spirit and energy of the plant from which they are extracted. They are normally extracted by steam distillation, which makes them around 70 per cent stronger than the plants or herbs from which they are derived.

We all react to smell, and different essential oils can soothe, relax or uplift us. Some also have strong cleansing properties, which can help to clear negative energies from the home.

Lavender is a good oil for general cleansing. It is believed to be the equivalent of neutral chi so can really help to shift stubborn energy, such as predecessor energy, which is imprinted on a building by previous occupants. Lime, orange, lemongrass or peppermint oils are good for stimulating the atmosphere. For general purification, the essential oils to use are juniper, sage, pine or eucalyptus.

Finally, it is important that you like the aroma of the oils that you choose to mist with. It is always more effective and enjoyable to work with a scent that you really like.

Using the oils

Add a few drops of your chosen essential oil to a mister bottle filled with water and shake well. If you want to mist regularly, change the oil every couple of days, or keep the solution in a dark glass atomizer, as plastic can affect the oil's properties.

Stand still for a moment and close your eyes to set your intent for what you want the oils to achieve, and how you want the negative energies to be released. Then start at the door of the room to be cleansed and walk around it, spraying all around, paying particular attention to corners. Work your way through any other rooms that need cleansing. To bring about a dramatic change in energy, spray every day for a week, and then once a week as a top-up. If you're using lavender oil to deal with difficult predecessor energy, it is a good idea to spray every room every day for 28 days, as this represents a complete cycle of chi.

To give yourself a quick boost, fill a small glass atomizer with water and one or two drops of your favourite essential oil. Mist around your head and body to revitalize your skin and to cleanse your aura.

CLAPPING

This is a very simple, but effective, technique for dispersing energy blockages and making shifts in your life. Think how clapping uplifts the atmosphere in a theatre at the end of a performance.

Relax and set your intent for what you want to happen or change in your home. Stand with your feet slightly apart. Start in one corner: use small, quick claps to test the quality of the energy and larger, louder claps to shift energy. The claps should sound crisp and clear if the energy is good; if they are muffled or dull, it normally means that the energy is poor. To get rid of this dead energy, clap up and down in the corner, visualizing the energy clearing as you do it. Move on round the room, making small claps, until you get to another corner that needs clearing. You can also 'clap out' cupboards, or work around electrical equipment to disperse the static electricity it generates.

Follow the same procedure in other rooms that need cleansing. When you have finished, rinse your hands under running water to remove any negative energy that may have clung to you. Repeat the clapping technique regularly to prevent any build-up of stale energy.

Clapping is a simple room cleansing technique, where you clap all around the room to lift stale energy.

INCENSE

If you walk into churches or temples in different parts of the world, you will often notice the pleasant, smoky aroma of incense burning. Incense sticks are easy to use and quickly raise the vibrational level of the energies in a room. There are different types of incense available – choose carefully because those made from synthetic substances may not have any effect on the energy in a room, or may even lower it. For powerful space-clearing, it is best to combine incense with another technique (see page 18).

The smell of incense also affects our senses. Hand-rolled varieties made from natural oils, gums, herbs and spices and other ingredients work well.

Using incense

If you are combining the use of incense with another space-clearing method such as misting with essential oils, just light an incense stick, place it in a holder and leave it smouldering in the background.

If you are using incense on its own, close your eyes, concentrating hard, and set your intent for that particular room or your home in general. Put the incense in a holder to carry around, light it, blow it out so that it starts smoking and, starting at the door, slowly walk around the room wafting the smoke with your hand, concentrating on corners and dark areas.

Repeat in other rooms, or set the incense on a side surface and leave it to burn out. Make sure it is positioned safely. Never leave burning materials unattended.

SALT

For centuries, salt has been used by different cultures to cleanse and purify negative energies, because of its ability to absorb impurities from the air. Salt is particularly good for enhancing other space-clearing techniques (see page 18) rather than just being used on its own. Rock or sea salt, kept in a sealed container, is best.

Salt for space-clearing

Sprinkle lines of salt across every doorway, or place bowls of salt in corners and in the middle of rooms for deeper cleansing. Or, toss salt in the four corners of a room and anywhere that you sense energy is stuck. Leave it for 24 hours, then remove it or sweep it up. If the energies in a room seem to have come to a complete standstill, renew the salt bowls every day for about a week.

MAKING A HOME ALTAR

When you have cleansed the energies in your home, you may want to create a special place to use for quiet contemplation or meditation for a short time each day. Here you can put a small altar or shrine to help you get in touch with your spiritual side. Start by creating a focal point on the altar – this can be a representation of a religious deity, such as a Buddah, a photograph of a natural place that inspires you, for example, or a picture of a person who helps you to connect spiritually. Include a favourite crystal, fresh flowers, and burn a candle and your favourite incense for a positive ambience whenever you use the altar. Set up the altar in a spare room or corner or, if you can't leave it on display, place on a tray and store in a cupboard until needed.

Burning incense in a living room, for example, will bring in a wonderful aroma and dispel a bad atmosphere or any negativity after an argument.

Clutter Hotspots

The way your home looks reflects your personality. So, if it is disorganized and full of clutter, the way you run your life will be similar. If you have a family, you can't blame the disorder on them because they are also a reflection of you. Many of your rooms may be overloaded with junk (see pages 32–79), but there are also certain areas, which if allowed to become overcrowded with clutter, can symbolically restrict you from enjoying life.

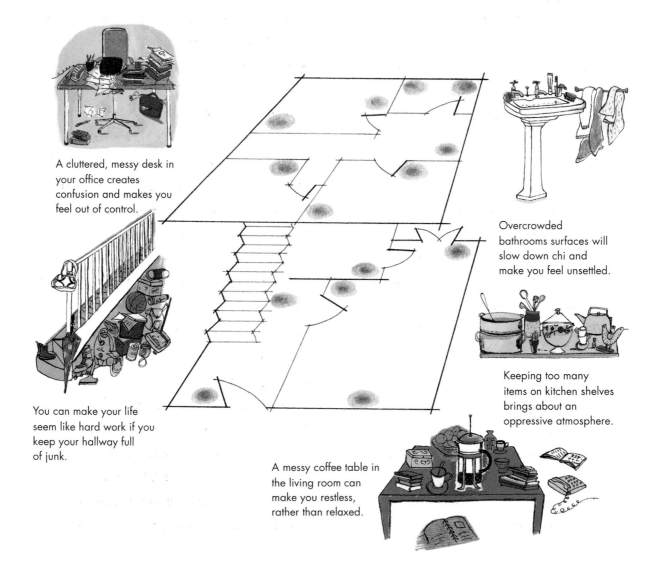

A cluttered, messy desk in your office creates confusion and makes you feel out of control.

You can make your life seem like hard work if you keep your hallway full of junk.

A messy coffee table in the living room can make you restless, rather than relaxed.

Overcrowded bathrooms surfaces will slow down chi and make you feel unsettled.

Keeping too many items on kitchen shelves brings about an oppressive atmosphere.

THE ENTRANCE AND HALLWAY

This is considered to be the 'mouth' of the home, where guests and friends enter and get their first impressions of where you live. It needs to be a bright, well-lit, welcoming environment that encourages chi to enter positively and meander through all the rooms in your home. All too often, this area is crowded with children's paraphernalia, shoes and bags, boxes and newspapers which make the energy slow and sluggish. If you have a pile of items stacked right by the entrance, it symbolizes life becoming a real struggle, with any new opportunities being barred.

ATTICS AND LOFTS

These are the places where we tend to store our past. These areas are therefore often full of mementoes and memorabilia that just make us look back and restrict us from making progress in life. By having a big clear-out you will feel unburdened, problems will no longer hang over you, and all your aspirations for the future will stop being restricted.

BASEMENTS

Not everyone has a basement area, but if there is one in your house, the likelihood is that it is jammed full of unwanted or unused paraphernalia. This area symbolizes your past and is believed to be linked to your subconscious mind. If it is brimming with junk, it represents things in your past that you have not addressed, or problems that you have been meaning to resolve for some time. It is really important to keep the basement well ordered, because if it is neglected, it can have a detrimental effect on you, making you feel miserable, lethargic and lacking a clear direction in life. If you feel weighed down by the troubles of the world, it could be that clutter lurking in the basement is the cause of this feeling of immobility.

THE BACK DOOR

This is where everything leaves your home and is therefore the symbolic organ of excretion. So if the area is full of junk, the analogy is that your home will become constipated, so it is important to keep it clear.

CORRIDORS AND PASSAGEWAYS

It is essential that chi flows easily through corridors to enable it to reach the upstairs or other parts of your home, so again any clutter will inhibit this process and should always be removed – common hotspots are either side of doorways and in wall recesses, so pay attention to these areas. If corridors and passageways are crowded, these energy conduits of the home will create feelings of restriction and an inability to progress in life.

The declutter plan

Before you start work on the plan, you need to assess what to keep or move, what to throw out and what to give away. If you feel reluctant to do this, persevere, because clearing out rooms or spaces is therapeutic. It will release old energies and bring in fresh possibilities.

You may find that you have confused feelings about why you are so attached to certain objects that seem to have no further use in your life. Think about how you regard your space, consciously and subconsciously, and how you can avoid letting your rooms or possessions take control of you in the future.

You do not have to throw everything out when you have your clear-out. In this bathroom, attractive storage baskets cleverly hold miscellaneous products.

ASSESSING YOUR JUNK

Now this is difficult. Go around your home with a pen and pad and note down your main junk areas, marking if they are large or small piles. Highlight the ones that irritate you the most, and start there first. Also pay attention to cluttered areas revealed by the Pa Kua (see page 14). If your career has been suffering and your career sector is full of rubbish, clear it out and see how your work life improves. Start slowly, tackling a cupboard or a room at a time, or the task will be too overwhelming.

BAG IT

Get five heavy-duty rubbish or garbage bags, or some strong cardboard boxes. Label the first bag 'junk' (all unwanted articles to go to the dump), the second bag 'charity shop or friends' (useful items you've grown bored with, but which other people might like, or which could be sold), the third bag 'things to be repaired or

It can be tempting to hide away unwanted goods or presents in suitcases, but this just brings about stagnancy in this area.

altered' (also include items for renovation) and the fourth bag 'things to sort and move' (useful articles that need a home). Fill a fifth bag with transitional items you can't quite let go of yet (keep for six months: if you miss them, they can be reinstated, if not, get rid of them).

With clothes, be tough, and keep only those you enjoy wearing and put on regularly – probably only a small percentage. Try on the ones you're not sure about, and if they don't fit or you dislike them, get rid of them. Also make a conscious decision never again to buy anything that you're not absolutely happy with.

JUNK CHECKLIST

It's categorized as junk if:
- it's broken and cannot be fixed;
- you dislike it every time you look at it;
- it was an unwanted present;
- it's an outmoded style or doesn't fit.

It's not junk if:
- you look at it with love and good feelings;
- it's something you really enjoy using;
- your work is helped by it.

Where the Spirit Rests

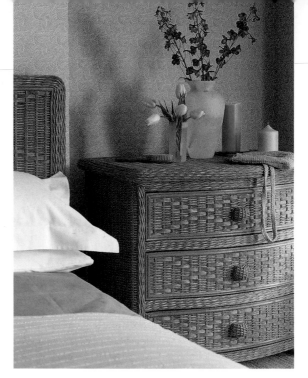

A bedroom is a personal haven, a place for letting go of the worries of the day. Here we want to feel nurtured, and be able to regenerate our mind, emotions and spirit. It is a sanctuary for sleeping, reading, dreaming, making love, and sharing any secrets or upsets. The room therefore should be calm and tranquil.

Wicker storage units blend in with the calm feeling of the bedroom. However, keep fresh flowers out the room as they drain energy.

ENERGY GRIDLOCK

Chi moves into the messy bedroom and is held back from reaching the window by the crowded wardrobe and the chair full of clothes. Chi entering by the window is slowed to the door by junk under the bed, a full dressing table and an overcrowded bookcase.

KEY: A chi enters; B overloaded wardrobe; C overladen chair; D chi leaves; E chi comes in window; F clutter under bed; G overstacked dressing table; H full bookcase; I chi leaves

ENERGY FREEWAY

Chi goes into the neat bedroom, travelling easily around the cleared wardrobe and chair and out the window. Chi comes in the window and meanders through the empty under-bed space, over the clear dressing table, and past the neat bookcase to leave the room.

KEY: A chi enters; B clutter removed from wardrobe; C empty chair; D chi leaves; E chi comes in window; F no clutter under bed; G solid, supportive headboard; H soft lighting from rounded lamps; I natural wooden flooring; J ordered dressing table; K tidy bookcase with minimal books; L chi leaves

The chi energy that flows through this area is very yin (passive) and will want to meander lazily. If your bedroom is crammed with too many items, the flow of chi will be hindered, denying you the relaxation and rejuvenation you seek. Clutter may also reveal the state of your love life. Is there a subconscious desire to keep a partner out of your life? Or does it reflect a chaotic marriage?

THE ENERGY TRAPS

Storing too much in the bedroom disturbs the harmonious flow of chi – so be firm with yourself.

Clothes: Are your wardrobes and drawers bulging with clothes? Most of us wear only 20 per cent of our wardrobes. If you can't throw clothes away, you can stay too attached to the past. Piles of discarded clothes create stagnant energy, so hang up your clothes each night and avoid sleeping with a laundry basket in the bedroom – yesterday's clothes give out dead energy.

Under the bed: It is tempting to store things under the bed, but if you do, these items will create 'stuck' energy. Your bed should be a place that encourages good health and romantic happiness, but sleeping over this heaviness can bring restless sleep and may disrupt your love life.

On top of wardrobes: Suitcases, bedding and boxes teetering on wardrobes will feel oppressive and affect your sleep, sometimes causing you to wake with a headache. Their looming presence may cause sluggishness and a reluctance to get up.

The dressing table: De-junk cosmetics clutter. Discard those extreme lip and nail colours – you won't fall in love with them one day – along with virtually empty lotion and perfume bottles. Leave only fresh products that you use regularly.

A personal sanctuary

First assess the room. Do you like its colour and energy, and feel that it cossets you? Your bedroom needs to reflect your future dreams.

MAKING SPACE FOR LOVE

If you want a partner, are you really allowing room for one to enter? You may also be subconsciously tying yourself to a past

A heaving wardrobe full of too many unworn clothes can keep you too linked to your past. Dispense with what you don't need to make your 'capsule wardrobe' which can be neatly stored away as above.

relationship, if your room contains mementoes from your last partner. New lovers will absorb this energy and feel rejected by it. Also, sleeping in a bed that a long-term partner has slept in will still contain his or her energies. Change the bed, the mattress, or at least buy new bed linen. If you live with a partner, assess the room to see if it reflects both of you; a troublesome relationship will normally be mirrored back at you. Remove, or at least cover at night, televisions, computers and mirrored wardrobe doors as they are too yang. If you're happy on your own, appraise your room to see if it is a sensuous niche. Does its contents show where you are at, or where you want to be?

COLOUR, MOOD AND LIGHTING

The vibrational energy that comes from your bedroom colours profoundly affect you and may make you feel negative. Good feng shui colours are shades of red – orange, soft pinks and apricot shades promote sensuality. Pastel blues, greens and lavender are calming and create a feeling of serenity.

Think carefully about lighting. Dimmer switches create a softer mood, while rounded bedside lamps give a warm glow for night reading. Flickering candles add romance; incense, or the scent of geranium from an aromatherapy burner creates fragrant relaxation. Put out all candles before sleeping.

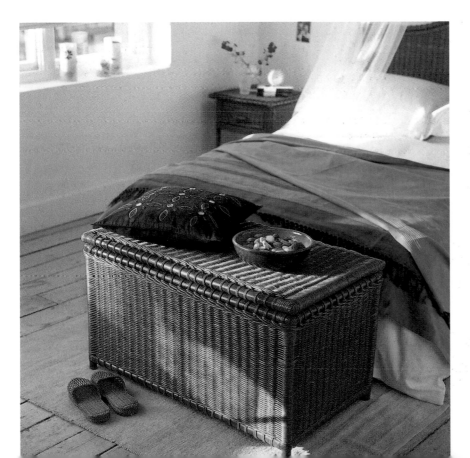

Junk that is thrown under the bed becomes stuck energy and can affect your health (top left). Clear out unnecessary goods and store your essentials in this blanket box, left. Place easily moveable items on top so that you can have access to its contents. A natural wood flooring encourages a good flow of chi.

Ordered bliss

Now you have rationalized your bedroom possessions, you need to look at how best to store your loved ones away to give you the peaceful atmosphere that is so needed in this

By planning in adequate shelving units that will hold shirts, jumpers, T-shirts, tops and other clothing you can make your bedroom a serene and well-ordered environment.

room. Study the room and see if there are any alcoves where you could fit an extra slimline unit. What you are trying to achieve is clean, ordered surfaces and tidy wardrobes so that the chi entering the bedroom flows smoothly.

STORAGE SOLUTIONS

Clothes and shoes: Look at what you have left: is it really now a 'capsule' wardrobe of your favourite items? Separate summer and

BEDROOM CLUTTER CHECKLIST

If your room is a clutter nightmare, search through everything, making your five distinct piles (see page 31).

◆ Clothes and shoes: empty your wardrobes and drawers, rationalizing what you really love to wear – and what you don't.

◆ Jewellery: remove broken items and pieces hardly worn.

◆ Cosmetics, lotions, perfumes and aftershaves: are these congealed or virtually finished?

◆ Bedding: is this piled on top of the wardrobe? Store elsewhere, and throw out old or torn linen.

◆ Books and magazines: be ruthless and keep to a minimum. Too many books in the bedroom is not good feng shui.

◆ Boxes of old sports gear, broken appliances and general clutter: if scattered around the room and under the bed, throw out now, or store properly elsewhere.

winter clothes and store those that are not currently used in a wardrobe in the spare room, or in a suitcase. If you have only one bedroom, see if your are making best use of the space – tall, wicker or rattan-style units with several shelves come in different sizes and fit well in recessed corners. They can easily store jumpers, tops, shirts, T-shirts or shorts.

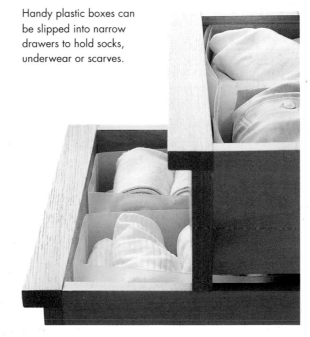

Reassess your wardrobe, or plan newly-fitted ones – can you fit in tiered racks for your shoes, or maybe canvas or mesh hanging racks if you have more hanging space? Jumpers and shirts can also be stored in larger hanging racks. If your wardrobe has shelves, fit in different-sized Perspex boxes to readily see all your stored goods or use multiple hangers to maximize your hanging space. Spare socks, tights, underwear, or ties in boxes can slot in drawers, or be safely placed in partitioned boxes on shelves.

Linen and bedding: Bulky duvets, pillows and bed linen can be hidden in blanket boxes or wicker baskets at the foot of the bed.

Cosmetics and jewellery: Regularly-used cosmetics can be stored upright in neat Perspex boxes and compartments, or placed in several small woven baskets. Sort jewellery into tiered or oriental-style boxes for easy access.

Books and magazines: Keep only one or two current magazines here and minimal books. Place favourite books on a small bookshelf or in a bedside cabinet.

Miscellaneous items: Don't store them in a drawer unit under the bed; keep elsewhere or in a stacking unit in the wardrobe.

Handy plastic boxes can be slipped into narrow drawers to hold socks, underwear or scarves.

Peace and Stimulation

Your children's bedroom is their own special place. As well as being somewhere to sleep, it is their refuge from the world, where they can play games, read, give rein to their creative abilities, settle down to their homework, hang their favourite posters, entertain friends and listen to music.

Although primarily for rest, the room is also an area where children need stimulation for homework and hobbies, so it benefits from positive chi energy. If their bedroom is overcrowded with unloved toys, sports gear or school items, the flow of chi will be hampered and this will make children unable to think clearly or to act in a positive way.

THE ENERGY TRAPS

Children are notoriously messy, often leaving toys and books strewn across the floor. But this trail of chaos disrupts the atmosphere and can disturb their sleep, so cajole them to tidy up on a regular basis.

Play or work areas If these are an explosion of cars, dolls, games, CDs, computer games and schoolwork, it will distort chi and prevent children getting good-quality sleep.

Overloaded cupboards If the doors will not shut because of all the goods stacked inside, a feeling of oppression will permeate the room (see page 20). Children may also subliminally worry that everything will fall out on top of

ENERGY GRIDLOCK

Chi moves into the children's messy bedroom and is stopped by an overladen cupboard. Its route to the window is further hampered by clothes and toys on the floor and clutter under the beds. Chi entering through the window is restricted on its way to the door by a crowded play table and books and clothes strewn on the floor.

KEY: A chi enters; B bulging cupboard; C scattered clothes and toys; D clothes and toys under beds; E chi leaves; F chi flows in window; G jumbled play table; H books and toys piled on floor; I chi leaves

Small hanging units add to the look of the bedroom and can display small painted toys.

ENERGY FREEWAY

Chi weaves into an ordered bedroom and flows evenly a round a cleared-out cupboard and stored toys, and through empty bed space to the window. Chi proceeds through the window and slides over an ordered play table and around the bare floor to the door.

KEY: A chi enters; B replanned cupboard; C bag for dirty clothes; D toys stored in stacking boxes; E no mess under beds; F rounded bedside lamps; G fabric wallhanging to slow chi; H chi leaves; I chi comes in window; J structured play table; K Anglepoise lamp for schoolwork; L cleared floor clothes; M chi leaves.

them – despite the fact that they created the situation in the first place.

Clothes Although children don't hang on to clothes because they are emotionally attached to them, they are adept at leaving them in scattered heaps, sources of stale energy that make the bedroom's atmosphere sluggish and dull.

Under the bed As with an adult's bedroom (see page 33), keep this area clear.

Keeping the children's bedroom tidy is a constant battle, so have plenty of tiered storage and make it a rule that all toys need to be put away at night.

A magical hideaway

Clearing up your children's bedroom will make you and them feel better (see checklist) – despite what they might say! But before you do this, pause and study the room. Appraise the furniture, the paint colour or wallpaper, the posters and pictures. Do they reflect your children as they are today, or is the room linked to the past? Have they been sleeping well, or possibly complaining of disturbed nights? Like an adult's bedroom, the children's room needs to be comfortable and somewhere that nurtures their developing personality and spirit.

THE RIGHT ATMOSPHERE

If the room looks chaotic, your children's behaviour and schoolwork may mirror this, with difficulty in focusing on projects, and failure to

Toys that are left scattered around the bedroom will make your children feel unsettled and restless. Tidy soft toys away in hanging storage bags or handy soft baskets, such as these (above).

CHILDREN'S BEDROOM CLUTTER CHECKLIST

Go through the room with your children, sorting out their toys and other equipment according to the five-bag system (see page 31).
◆ Toys and games: throw away everything that is broken and give away the unwanted or discarded items.
◆ Books: reserve the favourites and give away old titles to deserving causes such as hospitals.
◆ Computer games: see if you can sell or exchange the ones that have fallen from favour.
◆ Clothes: rationalize the clothes that are actually worn; pass on ones that are too small to younger children.

achieve the grades of which they are capable. The room's energy will also seem heavy, making them listless and lacking in enthusiasm.

If your children are sleeping in bunk beds, move them to separate beds as soon as you can, as the child on the bottom can feel restricted or compressed. In a teenager's room, a computer should be screened off so that its yang energies don't affect sleep. Avoid having a television in the bedroom, but if there is one, make sure it does not face the bed, and unplug it at night to reduce electromagnetic stress.

COLOUR, MOOD AND LIGHTING

Most children react strongly to colour. Bright colours and busy wallpaper designs can look good, but may be too stimulating for active children; soft pastel colours, purples, blues and greens will calm them. Give quieter children a

A chaotic bedroom (left, below) can give children problems with sleeping. Storage in bright primary colours (above) is always appealing and works well with children who are not too active. Pull-down blinds can conceal larger toys.

boost with pinks or oranges, and encourage creative children to thrive with shades of yellow.

Bedroom lighting is normally soft and ambient, but because of the mixed activities in children's rooms, good task lighting is important. Place an Anglepoise lamp in the study area, and install a sufficiently bright bedside lamp for reading.

Fabric or paper mobiles hung near the cot or bed, but not over it, are very relaxing for babies and toddlers. Restrict teenagers from having a vast collection of action-packed or violent posters, as they are too stimulating.

Stored benefits

Once you and your children have battled over their possessions, glance around their bedroom and see where you can create more storage. Don't forget that hanging units take up very little space. As this is a multi-activity room, for sleep and play, you need to leave clear floor space so that positive chi can move through freely.

Ingenious canvas hanging racks with numerous pockets can hold tiny toys and small pieces of clothing.

Painting a storage unit in a bright colour with a stencilled pattern can make it blend into the background.

STORAGE SOLUTIONS

Toys and games Children always have their favourites, so make sure that these are readily available. Try to get children to tidy up every night, explaining that they will feel better if they do so. Wooden chests or blanket-style boxes will quickly consume soft toys. Transparent or colourful plastic stacking boxes, which can stand on the floor or sit in a wooden unit, are great for building bricks, Lego pieces and small plastic toys. Fabric-covered boxes with lids are also useful and will stack on top of each other. For toy soldiers and other very small items, wooden units with several shallow drawers are ideal.

Canvas or cotton hanging sacks, suspended from hooks on the wall or wardrobes, will hold miscellaneous items. Games, which are more bulky, are best stacked on to wooden or metal shelving units.

Books Keeping too many books in the bedroom can be over-stimulating, so try and persuade your children to retain a select few here, and stow these neatly on bookshelves.

Computer games, disks, software and CDs This modern form of clutter is particularly prevalent in teenagers' rooms. It is hard to get teenagers to be tidy, but persuade them to stash disks and CDs in plastic boxes or on bookshelves, and put software disks and computer-related manuals out of sight in cupboards or on shelves.

Clothes and shoes Brightly patterned cotton hanging units hold several pairs of young children's shoes. For older children and teenagers, tiered shoe racks or hanging canvas or mesh racks fit inside wardrobes (see page 37). If you are replanning the room, think about installing fitted wardrobes with good hanging space and several shelves so that sweatshirts, T-shirts, jumpers and other items can be piled here, perhaps within pull-out plastic boxes. Again, make the most of hanging space with multiple skirt and trouser hangers (see page 37).

Discourage children from leaving clothes on the floor at night – clothes should be hung up, or placed in a canvas sack or laundry basket.

Bright plastic storage boxes on wheels hold a lot and can be easily moved around the bedroom. Do not regularly store them under the bed as this can cause disturbed sleep.

A Nurturing Place

Often considered the 'heart' of the home, the kitchen is where the family gather to eat, catch up on news and relax. It should be a warm and cosy environment, where everyone feels cocooned by its comforting ambience, and where senses are stimulated by wonderful, aromatic cooking smells.

The kitchen has become a room of many other functions too: children do their homework, adults steal half an hour to read a newspaper or book, and friends drop in for a chat and a coffee. And because this is the room where the family is fed and nurtured, the energy that moves through it needs to be positive and very yang. Cluttered work surfaces, fridge freezers, cupboards and floors will block chi flow, preventing the balance and harmony that is required.

THE ENERGY TRAPS

If you can never find that spice jar or bag of flour that you want because your cupboards are overstocked, or if you are constantly searching for the right kitchen accessory on your crowded worktops, a good clear-out is well overdue.

Good feelings of warmth and contentment should abound in a kitchen area. Keeping surfaces clear and having enough shelving and kitchen units will promote a good flow of energy.

ENERGY GRIDLOCK

Chi comes into a crowded kitchen and its progress towards the window is hindered by too much stored on cupboards, a full rubbish bin and full sink. The smooth movement of chi through the window to the door is stopped by crowded shelves and a messy floor.

KEY: A chi enters; B overstacked cupboards; C overflowing bin; D cluttered sink; E chi leaves; F chi comes in window; G overladen shelves; H crowded worktops; I littered floor; J newspapers; K chi leaves

Cupboards and kitchen units Overloading these will create a very oppressive atmosphere. Check use-by dates of packaged goods – if they have expired, you are allowing negative energies to enter this area. Stale energy is also created by unwanted or cracked utensils.

Work surfaces If you fill your worktops with too many utensils, gadgets, storage jars and other kitchen items, chi will be slowed down and this can adversely affect how you feel when cooking and eating in the kitchen.

Rubbish bins An overflowing bin creates negative energy and will seriously block energy flow, so empty it regularly.

ENERGY FREEWAY

Chi flows easily into a tidy kitchen, around cleared rubbish, over a clean sink and out of the window. Chi comes in the window and can freely move over neat shelves, around an ordered bin and tidied floor and out of the door.

KEY: A chi enters; B cleared cupboards; C empty sink; D chi leaves room; E chi comes in window; F structured shelves; G energizing plant; H empty, hidden bin; I hanging utensils; J empty floor; K chi leaves

Fridges and freezers These should always be full of food to symbolize the family's good health and wealth, but again, keep an eye on use-by dates, because storing expired goods could be very detrimental to the family's welfare.

Appliances Positive energy is given off by electrical equipment in the kitchen, but if broken appliances are left to fester on worktops, they will bring about energy blockages that will affect the room's happy atmosphere.

The floor area Bottles, newspapers and other items stacked haphazardly on the kitchen floor will look untidy and also make the flow of chi very sluggish.

A place of nourishment

Removing food that is no longer fresh from the kitchen and getting appliances mended will make you feel better (see checklist), but you'll need to tune in to the atmosphere, too. Do you like the room, and does its energy embrace you? Or do you feel irritated because work surfaces are cluttered and the cupboards are a mess?

Crowding too much kitchenware on open shelves (above) creates distraction and disturbance, so clear out what's not needed and display attractive glasses, crockery and storage jars (left).

If your cupboards contain enough packaged goods to keep you going for years, then you are missing out on the nurturing environment your family needs. Why are you hoarding so much food – are you subconsciously worried that you will not have enough? Does it stem from a childhood where food was restricted? Try and keep a more sensible stockpile. Inspect the cooker If the burners are clogged, you will restrict positive Fire energy, reduce the benefit you get from your food, and maybe inhibit your wealth potential. If the cooker is positioned right next to the sink or fridge/freezer, this produces a conflict between Fire and Water, which will disrupt the atmosphere of the room. Avoid this by placing a wood or metal unit between them to create a barrier. If your kitchen table is under a beam, it will be affected by downward 'cutting' chi, which is bad feng shui. Cutting chi will also affect tables that are close to sharp corners, which can prove harmful. Both can cause conflict at mealtimes, so move the table away from the beam and block cutting chi with plants.

COLOUR, MOOD AND LIGHTING

A kitchen needs to be airy and inviting, so white works well here – to the Chinese, this symbolizes purity. The ideal kitchen location is in the east or southeast sector of the house (Wood), so if yours faces in this direction you can enhance it with shades of green (Wood) or blue (Water), because according to the relationship between the five elements, which operate in a cycle, Water produces Wood. Wooden flooring and units add natural warmth.

Be careful not to use a strong red in a South-facing (Fire) kitchen, because it will emphasize the element too strongly, although white and metal accessories can counter this.

Good lighting brings in positive yang energy, so add downlighters or spotlights, and use strip lighting under units to illuminate food preparation areas.

Messy sinks, overflowing bins and other rubbish upsets the harmony in the kitchen (above). Concealing the bin in a unit and storing other kitchen goods away neatly will make the room seem calm but inviting. White is a good kitchen colour as it symbolizes purity (left).

Streamlined stocks

If you're suffering from exhaustion, having ruthlessly battled through the kitchen evaluating what you really do and do not need, take a short break to think about how you can increase your storage options for all the items that are left. See if you have space for more cupboard units, shelves or wall units.

STORAGE SOLUTIONS

Packaged goods, sauces and tinned food If you have a fitted kitchen and packaged goods are still too numerous to store in the units, consider adding extra units. Slimline cupboards will take advantage of a small gap.

Crockery and glasses Make a feature of these by displaying them in an open-fronted unit in a kitchen or dining area. Pine dressers, wooden or painted units with glass doors also do the job.

Fruit and vegetables A good way of storing these quickly consumed foods is to pack them in plastic baskets, and push these into either an open-fronted or closed unit under the worktop. Wicker baskets also look good when used individually or stacked together and slid under worktops. When space is tight, fresh produce can be placed in metal mesh baskets hung from a hook in the wall or the ceiling. Alternatively, a chrome trolley with basket shelves is useful because it can be quickly wheeled out of sight.

Cleaning goods All too often these disappear into a dark jungle under the sink, and it's difficult to identify what's living there. One solution is to fit a wire container with different compartments, that slides in and out on runners. Or separate the items into different baskets or plastic boxes and stack on the shelves of the sink unit.

Utensils and gadgets On worktops, keep these to a minimum. House sharp knives in cutlery units or wooden knife blocks. Never hang knives on a magnetic rack, because the sharp points will create harmful cutting chi. Other utensils can be suspended from hooks on a rail, possibly positioned above the cooker. Saucepans or mugs can also be hung from rails if you have limited unit space.

Miscellaneous items A kitchen trolley is a useful object and can sit under a worktop or at the side of the kitchen when not in use. Its tiled or wooden top gives you an extra preparation surface, while bottles of wine, regularly used crockery, utensils or tea towels can be stored on the bottom. Many contain drawers or handy hanging rails.

Storage jars, preserves and pasta jars These are good candidates for display, so clear them from worktops and place on simple open shelving. You can put up narrow shelves or racks to hold all your spices, making them easily accessible, and liberating some space in your cupboards.

Appliances Only leave out the ones that you use regularly, such as the toaster, the electric kettle and coffee machine. Store other items such as the iron, liquidizer, juicer and food processor in deep drawer units, or in cupboards with deep shelves.

KITCHEN CLUTTER CHECKLIST

Go through all your cupboards, sorting out items according to the five-bag system (see page 31).

◆ Packaged goods, sauces and tins of food: check for stale goods and those past their use-by date and throw out.

◆ Bottles, newspapers, old cartons and carrier bags: recycle these items, and take to the recycling centre regularly. Keep carrier bags for re-use.

◆ Appliances: if an appliance is broken, get it fixed or dispense with it.

◆ Rubbish bins: try to empty daily as they breed stagnancy in an otherwise positive area.

◆ Under the sink: sort through cleaning products and materials and only keep those you use regularly – get rid of impulse buys that have never been used.

◆ Fridge freezer: check each shelf, removing items that aren't fresh and out-of-date products.

◆ Work surfaces: minimize utensils and recycle glass storage jars.

When you have thrown out the kitchen goods that are not needed, display pleasing products such as storage jars and vinegars and oils on open shelving.

The 'Mouth' of the Home

The front entrance and hallway of your home are the first places friends and visitors see when they call around. It reflects your personality – a place of joyous welcomes and sad farewells. From here you view the world from both the inside and outside. The hall should be bright and welcoming – an area that invites people in.

Chi, the beneficial energy that creates balance and harmony, enters through the front door – the 'mouth' of the home – fulfiling the same function as food entering our bodies. Chi needs to flow in strongly and positively without obstruction, so cut back any overgrown plants or trees around the doorway, because they will inhibit its movement. If, once it enters the home, it has to struggle around items such as boxes, pushchairs and an overflowing coat rack, the symbolic meaning of this is that you are finding life hard work.

ENERGY GRIDLOCK

Chi comes through the front door, is obstructed by objects behind the door, and is prevented from moving up the stairs by blockages. Chi going down the hallway is restricted by too many items and a bulging cupboard.

KEY: A chi enters; B boxes and shopping trolley; C notes on mirror; D chi goes up stairs; E obstacles on stairs; F chi goes down hallway; G overladen coat rack; H bike and other clutter; I cupboard full of junk; J chi leaves

ENERGY FREEWAY

Chi meanders into an ordered home, is slowed by the wind chime and moves effortlessly around a storage unit and clean mirror and up well-lit, cleared stairs. Chi going down the hallway flows around a neat coat rack and umbrella stand, along the empty floor, past plant which slows chi, and ordered cupboard.

KEY: A chi enters; B put wind chime over door; C storage unit and key holder; D mirror; E well-lit, inspirational pictures; F cleared stairs; G chi goes down hallway; H organized coat rack; I healthy plant; J empty floor; K rationalized cupboard; L chi leaves

The hallway is the first place that visitors see when they enter your home, so it needs to be uncluttered with a bright and inviting atmosphere and good lighting.

THE ENERGY TRAPS

An overcrowded hallway, where everybody sees fit to leave miscellaneous items scattered haphazardly all over the floor, will soon start to wear you down. You may feel your life is losing direction, and because chi can't enter this area properly, you will be restricted in everything you are trying to do, and new opportunities will be blocked.

The porch and hallway Tripping over old umbrellas, golf clubs, bikes, pushchairs, boxes, muddy shoes or wellington boots will cause constant annoyance and irritation. The hampered flow of chi will disturb the atmosphere, making visitors uneasy as they enter your home.

Hallway table or desk Stacks of local newspapers, junk mail and unpaid bills are stale energy and will slow down your progress in life.

Alcoves These are dangerously shaped for attracting clutter and so forming negative energies – so beware!

Stairs If you leave files, books and papers on the stairs, you will restrict the energy flow through the home and feel a heaviness every time you go upstairs.

Under the stairs If this is your 'black hole' where every possible item of junk and DIY items gravitate towards, their stale energy will seep out into other areas of your home. This can make the people who live there feel lethargic and depressed.

HALLWAY CLUTTER CHECKLIST

Rationalize what to keep and what to throw away, making piles to put into your five-bag system (see page 31).

◆ Shoes, wellingtons, walking shoes, sports shoes: return to the wardrobe, or to the dustbin if they are worn out.

◆ Junk mail, newspapers, bills, keys: sort through the piles, then file the essentials and recycle or dispense with the rest.

◆ Coat rack: check through all the jackets and coats, decide what is currently used and throw away or store the remainder elsewhere.

◆ Bikes, pushchairs, golf clubs, sports gear: if these are now redundant, sell or give away; alternatively, find good storage solutions.

◆ DIY goods: get rid of dried-up filler, paints, old glues or other out-of-date products that may be lurking under the stairs.

The inner world

Removing obstructions from your hall and entrance will help you to move on in life (see checklist), but also study its overall atmosphere. Is it bright and inviting, or dark and restricting? Does it echo how you feel about your life?

HALL LAYOUT PROBLEMS

If your entrance and hallway are a mess, ask yourself why you are stopping good things coming into your life. See how your door opens – does it get blocked by clutter inhibiting the chi? Look at the geography of the area. According to feng shui, a staircase should not start directly opposite the main door, and a curved staircase is often preferable to one that is straight. If your stairs do face the door, hanging wind chimes over the front door will help slow down the flow of energy.

COLOUR, MOOD AND LIGHTING

A warm, welcoming light outside and good ceiling lighting inside will encourage people in. To expand a narrow hallway, hang a mirror on a side wall. To lead people to the first floor, put up well-lit inspirational pictures along the stairs. As this area needs to be welcoming, soft pastel blues, greens, pinks or shades of white or cream are soothing colours for walls and paintwork.

Left: Shades of white or soft pastels can help to expand a narrow hallway. This area need not be stark, when you have removed any clutter, hang inspiring pictures, fit interesting lights and add chairs, tables or small storage units.

Left: Too many coats, jackets and scarves can overwhelm coat racks, so give away those you don't need and choose a functional style that works for you and your family.

STORAGE SOLUTIONS

After your major clear-out, muse about new storage solutions that will blend with the pleasant ambience of this area. An interesting oriental pot can hold umbrellas.

Shoes, wellingtons and sports shoes

A tiered plastic or metal shoe rack in the porch or by the front door will hold several pairs of shoes. Or, install neat wooden shoe cabinets with hinged drawers in the hall, or a tall, slim cabinet that combines sloping shelves for shoes at the bottom with other useful shelves above.

Hats, coats and jackets Choose a coat rack with rails for hanging items, and a flat area on top for hats and scarves. Or, place a conventional coat stand in an unused corner. There are also slimline units with outer hooks and sliding doors concealing shoe shelves.

Junk mail, bills and keys A desk or low wooden storage unit with drawers can house these items. Hang keys on the wall behind for easy access. Clip interesting flyers together and file in drawers or cardboard magazine files. Put bills in a plastic folder with compartments.

Bikes, pushchairs, sports gear and DIY items Preferably, store bikes in a garage or shed, or under the stairs. Suspend a pushchair from a strong hook under the stairs or in a hall cupboard; likewise hang golf clubs and sports gear. There are special under-the-stair units for open staircases, with different-sized plastic stacking units. These are ideal for DIY paraphernalia.

Sociability and Relaxation

The living room is the focal point of the home, where the family gathers to unwind from the relentless pressures of daily life. It is a room where lively conversations about the state of the country or the meaning of life can stretch long into the night. It is a special meeting place, where old and new guests are welcomed and entertained.

The living room is often multifunctional, with one area for relaxing, another for dining and a corner for a home office, from which the household is run and organized.

Although this is essentially a tranquil room, the living room is also a sociable place and needs a positive chi movement in order to keep

A well-planned seating layout in your living room adds to its appeal and conviviality. Making sure it is junk-free will aid energy movement and sociability.

ENERGY GRIDLOCK

Chi streams into the crowded living room and on its way to the window hits videos on the floor and struggles around a piled bookcase and coffee table. It is slowed by clutter behind the sofa, boxes of wine and a muddled cupboard. From the window to its exit through the door, it is restricted by the crowded table, furniture and floor.

KEY: A chi enters; B piles of videos; C overstacked bookcase; D messy coffee table; E piles of junk and CDs; F unwanted boxes; G too full unit; H chi leaves; I chi comes in window; J untidy table; K jumbled floor; L mess behind furniture; M chi leaves

conversations flowing and to create a good, uplifting ambience. If the room is cluttered or over-furnished, the energy will stagnate, engendering unsettled and restless feelings, rather than the desired feeling of contentment and relaxation.

THE ENERGY TRAPS

Finding a big piece of furniture barring your way when you enter your living room, or having to navigate round piles of newspapers, magazines and other paraphernalia, is at odds with the aim of creating a relaxing, sociable atmosphere, so you need to do some clearing and streamlining.

Behind sofas Your sofa can be a clutter magnet. If the area behind your sofa conceals a morass of discarded craft projects, unhung pictures, leaflets and packets of old photographs, you have created a brooding stagnancy behind you that will disturb you every time you sit down.

On bookshelves Symbolically, books are linked to your likes and beliefs, so if there are a lot of dusty old books sitting on the shelves, it indicates that you are becoming very set in your ways.

Overcrowded mantelpieces A vast assortment of ornaments, candlesticks, dishes and ashtrays looks unsightly and will induce a restless energy.

ENERGY FREEWAY

Chi enters the well-planned lounge, sweeping around the re-vamped TV storage unit and bookcase with a plant, around the empty coffee table and tidied furniture and floor to the cleared unit and out of the window. The chi that enters by the window streams over the polished table, over the clean floor and out the door.

KEY: A chi enters; B stacked TV unit; C tidy bookcase; D energizing plant; E hanging crystal to slow energy; F cleared furniture; G CD unit; H bare floor; I organized unit; J chi leaves; K chi enters; L extra storage unit; M empty table; N cleared floor; O chi leaves

Under coffee tables Overflowing piles of magazines will bring about a central area of stale energy that will slow down all the family.

Overstocked cupboards or units Stacks of old videos, records, CDs, cassette tapes and other items, piled haphazardly on top of each other, link you too much to your past, rather than your future. Chi will be very sluggish here, and actually make people reluctant to play music at all.

Drinks cabinet If, when you open the door, the first thing that you see is odd, cracked glasses and almost empty bottles of spirits, the mess and disorder will bring you down.

The comfort zone

Getting down to the task of refining your main living space and making it more homely is very rewarding, but before you start your clear-out (see checklist), take time to assess this area where you spend so much of your time, to see what it says about you. Does its décor and furnishings welcome you, or are they looking tired and shabby, maybe reflecting what you are secretly feeling about life? Are you keeping it cluttered and overcrowded as a symbol of your refusal to let changes happen in your life?

ROOM TO RELAX?

A cluttered living room will deter guests from lingering. If your room is like this, it may reveal a subconscious desire to keep people away.

Pay attention to the positioning of furniture: sofas and chairs are best placed in a semi-circle around a coffee table or in front of the fire so that they face each other, making it easy for people to chat. Never put chairs under a beam,

It is hard to relax in a room which is full of unloved and discarded items (left). Keep as little as possible on coffee tables (above) and display your favourite, loved possessions on attractive storage units.

Regularly go through your books and review what you really need as too many old ones can make you set in your ways (left). Place your favourite books and treasured artefacts that are left on well-lit shelving.

because the cutting chi that comes down from it can cause headaches. Sharp edges and pointed structures channel bad feng shui referred to as poison arrows. To avoid your suffering from the effects of these, furniture such as shelves with sharp edges can be obscured with trailing plants, while sharp-angled tables can be covered with cloth made from interesting fabrics. In a large living area, a dining area can be demarcated with shelving units or large sofas.

COLOUR, MOOD AND LIGHTING

Shades of cream or soft pastel colours create a relaxing ambience. Yellow will expand a room and helps to stimulate conversation. Alternatively, you could paint the room in relation to the room's element according to the Pa Kua. So if it faces north, for example, it should be blue, but if it faces south a shade of red is appropriate (see page 14).

Lighting is important in a living room to draw in good yang energy. Use uplighters or pendant lights for background lighting, lamps for mood lighting and spotlights for accent lighting on pictures, ornaments and plants. The soft, natural light of candles adds a special appeal. To promote a feeling of calm, wellbeing and harmony, burn fragrant incense or essential oils.

Structured tranquillity

Clearing out items from this room is never easy, but you will immediately notice an uplift in its energy when you do so. Walk around the room and decide how you can improve the storage of your remaining possessions. If you adore books and still have many left, appraise where you might fit in another shelving unit.

STORAGE SOLUTIONS

Books Consider building shelves into any unused alcoves – you can also put a cupboard underneath the shelves that will hold other miscellaneous goods. A wide, freestanding open wooden bookcase will hold many titles. Try to intersperse sections of books with ornaments to break up the solidity of its appearance. Buy a bookcase on castors so that it can be moved around easily, or used as a room divider for separating the dining and relaxation areas.

Take your CDs off the floor and house them in stylish wooden cabinets such as this one.

LIVING ROOM CLUTTER CHECKLIST

Work methodically through your living room items, making distinct piles to put into your five-bag system (see page 31).

◆ Books: be ruthless – keep the special ones, but sell the rest or give to charity shops or a hospital.

◆ Wallets of photographs: these create dull energy, so sort through them all and put the pictures that give you joy into frames or an album, then discard the rest.

◆ Magazines and newspapers: cut out the interesting articles and keep them for reference, then take the rest to a recycling centre.

◆ Old videos, records, CDs and cassette tapes: sell what you can; discard any old tapes.

◆ Ornaments: ask yourself why you are keeping gifts or old family items that you don't like. Retain only those that you really love and give away the rest.

◆ Glasses, bottles of spirits: glasses create positive energy, but not if damaged. Throw out those that are cracked or chipped and ditch bottles that are almost finished.

Photographs Go through these carefully, only keeping those that fill you with love and affection. The danger of hoarding a vast collection of old photographs is that it can link you too strongly to your past. Just keep a few happy pictures of past relationships and dispense with the rest. Make a montage in a glass clipframe of current photos of family and friends. Or display photos of loved ones or happy holidays in metal or wood frames in your relationship or fame areas (see pages 14–15) respectively. Place all other pictures in attractive albums and store neatly in a cupboard unit.

Magazines and newspapers These form an ongoing clutter problem that needs constant vigilance. Once you have cut out any articles you want for reference, keep current newspapers and magazines in a stylish magazine rack made from metal, wood or other combinations. One ingenious cast-iron style has hooped sides to store newspapers flat, allowing string to be put around them for easy removal to a recycling centre.

TV, videotapes, CDs and cassette tapes
Easy access is the key for these frequently used items. Feng shui practice dictates that it is preferable to cover a television when it is not in use as it gives off so much yang energy and

electromagnetic stress, so house it in a cupboard or TV unit with doors. Videotapes can be stored in a bottom drawer. Slimline CD units are available in different styles to blend in with your room's decor; wider units will hold up to 244 CDs. Freestanding metal shelving units are also a good solution for CDs and videotapes.

Ornaments Place on shelves with books, or display a favoured collection in an illuminated glass cabinet. Clever small cube units (open, with doors, or including shelves) can be mixed and matched to display ornaments, vases, favourite books and picture frames.

Glasses and bottles Glasses are very yang and add to the positive energy of the living room. Good-quality glassware looks stunning arranged in a glass cabinet with a wooden frame. Inbuilt downlighters really high-light the sparkle of the glasses.

Soft baskets can hold craft projects (left). Screens can divide multifunctional rooms (above). Candles add yang energy to the living room (right).

Purifying the Soul

Soaking in a hot, relaxing bath or reviving yourself with a quick shower can help you forget all the problems of the day. The bathroom is a place where you can close the door and escape from the outside world – a private retreat for cleansing the body and soul, and somewhere for meditation, contemplation and inspiration, where ideas are considered and new ones are born. It needs to be a warm and inviting environment where you want to linger – a place that cherishes you.

In a bathroom, water is constantly draining away, making it a very yin environment that is

Bathrooms are places where we can escape from the world, so need to be tranquil rooms with clear floors and surfaces.

prone to stagnation. A surfeit of furniture and messy, overcrowded surfaces will slow down chi energy and stop it circulating properly. The ensuing atmosphere will be stale and the room will make you feel restless and unsettled. In feng

ENERGY GRIDLOCK

Chi comes into the cluttered bathroom and is blocked by boxes of bathroom products, it then hits the crowded vanity unit and medicine cabinet and is further hindered by clothes on the floor and the mass of beauty items around the bath before it goes out of the window. The flow of chi from the window is interrupted by more products on the bath and towels on the floor before it exits the room.

KEY: A chi enters; B boxes of bathroom products; C crowded vanity unit; D overstocked medicine cabinet; E clothes on floor; F overladen bath; G chi leaves; H chi comes in window; I too many bath products; J wet towels; K chi leaves

ENERGY FREEWAY

Chi drifts into the well-planned bathroom and around the wicker storage unit and healthy plant, over the bare floor. It goes past the overhauled vanity unit and medicine chest, past an enhancing plant and candles and out of the window. Chi flowing through the window moves fluently over the smooth bath surfaces, over the mat and towel rail and exits out of the door.

KEY: A chi enters; B energizing plant; C tiered, natural bathroom unit; D re-worked vanity unit; E cleared medicine chest; F plant and candles for yang energy; G chi leaves; H chi comes in window; I natural blind; J products moved from bath; K cotton bathmat; L heated towel rail; M chi leaves

shui terms, bathrooms are not always viewed auspiciously, because water is also linked to money, and this room sees it running away. It is therefore preferable that it is not located in your wealth or career sector. However, they can still be pleasant environments.

THE ENERGY TRAPS

If you find it hard to get in and out of your bathroom because of all the units and baskets, or if you can never find your shampoo, conditioner or shower gel because they are buried under a mound of other toiletries, you need a thorough cleansing session.

Bathroom cupboards and vanity units

These are good for storage, but if they are packed full of beauty and bathroom items that constantly spill out when you open the doors,

making it hard to find what you want to use, you will feel irritated and frustrated.

Around the washbasin and side of the bath A plethora of bottles and tubes, which are guilty of leaving messy deposits in these areas, create a chaotic, disordered feel in a room that should be pleasant and calm. Consider why you feel you need so many.

On the floor Keeping a stock of toilet rolls and cleansers can be a good idea, but if they are stacked on the floor so that you constantly trip over them, they will cause annoyance.

Medicine cabinets Most medicines, tablets and creams have a short shelf-life, so check your cabinet to ensure that you don't have expired items. Don't keep a lot of unnecessary products that are rarely used – if you do, ask yourself why you are holding onto so many products that only link to ill-health.

A haven of peace

Removing superfluous goods from your bathroom will make you feel better (see checklist), but take a few moments to get a sense of the room that you normally take for granted. It mirrors part of your personality, so do you like what you see? If the paintwork is dirty or peeling, it may indicate a pattern of neglect that you are repeating in your life. Or does its disorder suggest discontentment in your life?

CREATING AN OASIS

Your bathroom should be an oasis where you can refresh body and mind, but if it is a mess, the chi (which is low here anyway) will struggle to work its way through. The stagnancy will drain your energy levels, making you feel constantly tired and listless, and lacking in enthusiasm for life.

COLOUR, MOOD AND LIGHTING

Bathrooms are relaxing rooms, but need to be fed with positive energy to counteract the damp, humid, slightly negative atmosphere that is

A bathroom cabinet which is packed full of bathroom products will always irritate you as you won't be able to find anything (left). Regularly remove what you don't need from the cabinet and maybe use baskets inside to maximize the space (below). Painting the bathroom green is very calming and aids digestion.

always present. The colour on the walls will also influence your mood. A soft green in a bathroom can aid digestion, while blue, linked to flowing rivers, seas and lakes, is seen to keep the water in the room flowing swiftly, which is beneficial.

BATHROOM CLUTTER CHECKLIST

Make your bathroom an enjoyable place to be by first forming your five bags of clutter (see page 31).

◆ Medicines: check all the use-by dates and throw out accordingly.

◆ Bathroom cleaners, toilet rolls: don't keep enough for an army, just retain a few extra toilet rolls and store your back-up collection elsewhere.

◆ Bath salts, oils, shower gels, shampoos and conditioners: are you hoarding a lot of samples? Start working through them, or throw them away. Get rid of any products that are old, dried up or nearly finished.

◆ Towels and bath mats: do you have more sets than you need? Are they torn, fraying or have they seen better days? If so, you know what to do.

Pinks and peaches are calming and soothing.

Healthy, round-leaved plants will give the room a lift, while using fragrant bath lotions or burning essential oil will clear any negativity. Mirrors bring in powerful energy, so position one over the washbasin, and always keep it clean and shining. If it becomes tarnished or cracked, replace it immediately as this is bad feng shui

and you could be adversely affected.

Soft, fluffy towels in pleasing pastel colours will counteract the harder lines of tiled surfaces and the ceramic bathroom suite.

Ceiling downlighters, and task lighting for shaving or applying make-up, will give the right level of brightness. Use scented candles in wall sconces, or safely positioned around the bath to bring in enticing Fire energy.

Leaving wet towels and dirty clothes around the bathroom will further stagnate the slow energy here (above). This bathroom cabinet (left) can take towels, mats or a small laundry basket and smaller accessories in the drawers.

Perfect serenity

After you have done a sweep of your bathroom and eliminated everything that's past its best, rethink the way you can best display and store all the essentials in this special room. Bathrooms are often littered with an assortment of bottles of various types of scented gunge, which tend to congregate untidily on window ledges and bath surrounds. The bathroom is often humid and steamy, slowing chi flow, so aim to keep surfaces clear so that the movement of chi is not hindered further.

Towels are better placed in a unit but can sit on shelves when clean and dry.

STORAGE SOLUTIONS
Bath and beauty products

Generally, these are very attractively packaged, so they look good on open shelving. But do not have too many products on show, just the ones that you regularly use. You can get hanging units to suspend from the shower pipework, which hold shampoo, shower gel, sponges and soap. Other styles have suction cups that stick to wall tiles. Metal hanging baskets, particularly in a verdigris style, can look stylish. Fit corner shelving into spaces that wouldn't otherwise be used. Glass shelving looks good, and is practical and easy to clean.

If you do your make-up in the bathroom, consider buying a unit with drawers that incorporate divided trays with sections for brushes, foundation, lipsticks and eyeshadows.

Medicines and first-aid kit

These are best hidden away neatly in a wall cabinet. Alternatively, use stacking baskets in a cupboard, or tiered wicker units with pull-out drawers (good for tight spaces).

Bathroom cleansers and other products

While these are all very necessary, and you may want them on hand rather than in a kitchen cupboard, they clutter and detract from

In a large bathroom area, build in as many storage cupboards as you can so that you don't have to leave many goods out. Flowers or plants can raise the chi here.

the room if they are left on view. If you lack space to store them, consider buying a vanity unit to fit around the washbasin. This will utilize the wasted space under the basin and give you at least two extra shelves for storing bulky items such as toilet rolls, cloths, bleach, disinfectant and bathroom cleaners.

Towels and bathmats Fluffy towels and accessories add a wonderful yin quality to the bathroom. As they are so tactile, extra towels can be put out on display in open units, possibly on glass shelves. Alternatively, they can go in glass-fronted units, or in plastic baskets contained in open modern chrome units, mixed in with other baskets of bathroom products (see above).

Creativity and Prosperity

Most of us spend more hours each day in an office environment than we do in our own homes. Even if we work from home, we usually shut the door on our outer family world so that we can get down to work. It is here that we give full rein to our talents for bringing wealth, prosperity and success into our lives. Clarity and concentration are essential for making the right decisions; we are constantly performing, juggling time and budgets. Here appraisal is constant – all the efforts we make are judged and assessed by bosses, co-workers and clients.

So, the room you work in should nurture you and your abilities – it should be a pleasant, well-lit, inspiring environment that makes you feel at ease and determined to achieve your best.

The flow of chi in an office must be strong and yang to encourage a positive attitude. If your desk is cluttered with numerous items and the floor is covered with boxes, reports and files, chi will get stuck and your creativity and decision-making skills will be blocked, causing you to work in a confused, disorganized way.

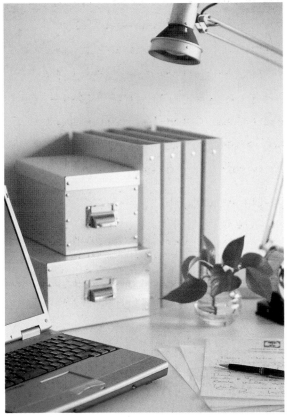

An ordered office environment will help you think clearly and make decisions more easily.

THE ENERGY TRAPS

As well as slowing down the chi, an overcrowded office area will restrict the pace of the business, causing upsets and misunderstandings about the current workload.

The desk Heaps of paperwork awaiting action, files that have not been put away and unpaid invoices create pools of stagnant energy, making you feel stressed, out of control and unproductive. If you can never find anything you need in your desk drawers because they are full of irrelevant office equipment, pens that don't work and old notes, this confusion will make you work sluggishly.

Filing cabinets When these are overfilled with redundant projects or contain details of bad clients, they make a negative space.

Floor area If it is an obstacle course of boxes, stacks of files, old reports, printer paper and other items, these will all restrict energy flow, making the office atmosphere dull.

Cupboards Bulging office cupboards can make the people feel oppressed and threatened.

Shelves A lot of out-of-date reference books, catalogues or brochures will just link the business to its past.

Computer Leaving old material on your machine will hold you back from progressing with new projects.

ENERGY GRIDLOCK

Chi proceeds into the jumbled office and is stopped by an overflowing wastebin, files and a full filing cabinet. It tries to move over a littered desk and windowsill before escaping out of the window. Chi streaming in through the window is restricted by too many books on the fax unit and boxes on the floor before leaving the room.

ENERGY FREEWAY

Chi moves into a spring-cleaned office and weaves easily around an emptied filing cabinet and stored files, over the ordered desk space and windowsill and out of the window. The flow of chi back through the window is encouraged by a healthy plant, an uncluttered fax unit and an empty floor area before leaving the room.

KEY: A chi enters; B littered bin; C box files on floor; D groaning filing cabinet; E disorganized desk; F piles of paperwork; G chi leaves; H chi comes in window; I stacks of books; J crowded box; K chi leaves

KEY: A chi enters; B cabinet with current files; C tidy box files; D supportive chair; E efficient desk space; F task light; G clear windowsill; H wooden blind; I chi leaves; J chi enters; K plant to boost atmosphere; L tidy fax unit; M cleared floor; N chi leaves

The work domain

Going through an office and throwing out what's not needed (see checklist) is hard work, so first take a few moments to view your working environment through different eyes. Does it make you feel claustrophobic? Do you feel happy working there, and does its colour and lighting work well, lifting your energy?

WORK ETHICS

To help you work well, the room's atmosphere must encourage productivity. Does the atmosphere feels slow and heavy? If so, it may be a reflection of a business that is run in a rather haphazard way. Consider how your business or the firm is doing. Has new work decreased or have orders dropped? A disorganized office will dramatically affect the smooth running of a business. Chi will have a problem working its way around the room, and you will feel this hindrance in everything that you attempt – people will always be engaged when you call, important appointments will be cancelled, or files will suddenly go missing.

If you work at home on your own, and find that you are often restless and unable to sit still or concentrate for long during your working day, it

Files, reports and other papers scattered on the floor will confuse your working practice, so have as many filing cabinets as you can. These Asian wooden ones are also attractive pieces of furniture.

may be because you are surrounded by clutter.

Check to see if cutting chi is coming from sharp corners or shelves and hitting your desk. If so, deflect it with healthy, green, round-leaved plants, or push books to the front of shelves to soften their hard edges. Fresh flowers will lift everyone's mood and raise the energy of the office. Always remember to empty all wastepaper bins daily so that you are not surrounded by pockets of stagnant energy.

The effects of electromagnetic stress from a computer can be alleviated by taking regular breaks and placing a clear quartz or rose quartz crystal next to it to soak up some of the negative emissions. A cactus called *Cirrus peruvianus* is also good for absorbing the emissions. Peace lilies, peperomias and dwarf banana plants help cleanse the atmosphere.

COLOUR, MOOD AND LIGHTING

Light creams, white or pastel colours will increase the space and airiness of an office, or the room can be painted according to the appropriate element (see page 14). Good overhead lighting is important, and daylight bulbs, although expensive, help reduce eyestrain as they are the nearest to the ultraviolet light we experience outside. Anglepoise desk lamps assist close reading and computer work.

Sunlight introduces warmth and yang energy, but can be blinding and create irritating glare on computers, even in winter, so venetian blinds at the windows are essential. To reduce glare, position your desk so that windows are at the side of it. If you cannot avoid glare, hang a faceted spherical crystal (see page 90) in the window to dispel the negative chi from the glare.

In a home office, ideally face south as this is your fame area. Always sit with your back to the wall, for support, and face the door.

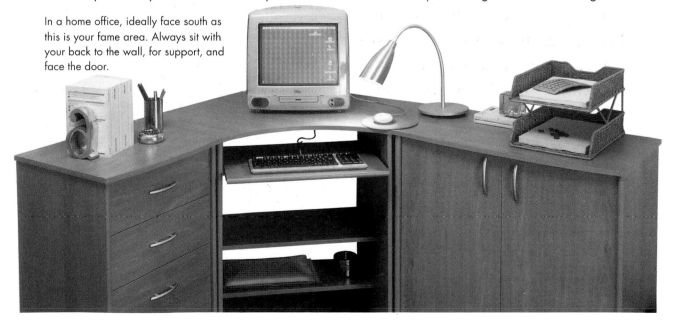

Successful placement

The position of your desk can affect your work efficiency and achievements. The best position, in feng shui terms, is in the corner that is diagonally opposite the main door of your office. You need to be able to see the door and who is coming into the room. If you sit with your back to the door, you will always feel threatened, or that other colleagues are betraying you. However, if sitting like this is unavoidable, you can hang a small mirror over your desk so that you see the door behind you reflected in it.

Your chair should always have a solid wall, rather than a window, behind it, because this gives you symbolic support. If you have no choice but to sit with a window behind you, then keep the blind down – doing this symbolizes a measure of support. Also, avoid sitting too close to the office door, because it will make you feel that you are unprotected and that you are losing control.

Tall, slim filing cabinets can be slotted into narrow spaces in the office.

SITING A HOME OFFICE

An ideal position for your home office (if you are running a business) is facing south, because this governs your fame area. Situate a home study to face the northeast, which relates to your education and knowledge area. If these positions are not possible, use your compass (see page 15) and place your desk in a south or northeast corner.

AN OPEN-PLAN OFFICE

When several members of staff share an open-plan office, it is better to get a feng shui consultant in to map it out and ascertain the best positions for people to sit. Alternatively, use the compass and Pa Kua and from your readings work out the most auspicious areas for computers, fax machines and filing cabinets. You can also follow some general guidelines. The most favourable position for the manager's office is farthest from the office door, so that he or she is apart from the bustle of the office, and is able to make decisions without distractions, promoting good control over the business. Do not place desks facing each other because this can cause confrontation between colleagues.

If your desk is constantly in a mess, you will work in a distracted, unstructured way and will be forever losing files, invoices and vital reports and notes. Try to address correspondence as soon as it comes in or make your comments and pass it on. The aim at the end of the day is to leave an empty, tidy desk – this is not always easy to achieve, but it is something to aim for.

Computer disks and fiddly stationery items such as staples, paperclips, erasers and pens and pencils can be put in this small unit (below).

OFFICE CLUTTER CHECKLIST

Although clearing out office clutter is slightly different from sorting out the home, you can still work through the five-bag system (see page 31).

◆ Files: sort through your filing cabinets and throw out redundant files, keeping only the current ones.

◆ Catalogues, reference magazines and brochures: send old ones for recycling.

◆ Reference books: keep up-to-date books with the latest information, and give the rest away.

◆ Reports: retain reference copies of old reports and shred the rest.

◆ Desk: transfer messages or Post-it notes to your diary, and junk any irrelevant pieces of paper crowding the desk.

◆ Computer: go through the hard disk and put disused programs, completed or abandoned projects and e-mails on a back-up disk or archiving system, or throw away.

Inspired filing

Now that you have started taking action in your home office or your place of work, by removing waste and clutter, you need to evaluate how to make better use of your space so that it doesn't become a mess again. See if there is room for more filing cabinets to consume paperwork or files stacked on the floor. Is it necessary to buy another cupboard for stationery? Perhaps an alcove can be utilized by building in more shelves for reference books.

Stationery trays need not be only metal or plastic but can also be made from natural fibres, which are especially good for chi movement (left).

If you do not have too many files, these storage boxes will be perfectly adequate (above).

STORAGE SOLUTIONS

Files If your company has numerous projects running at one time, with related files, it is worth installing tall, metal filing cabinets that feature several shelves of hanging files. Box files can be stored in smaller versions with deeper shelves. Alternatively, incorporate conventional metal filing cabinets with two, three or four pull-out drawers. To boost the Metal element, place these in the west of the office. In a home office, there is usually a less pressing demand for filing space, and attractive wooden or melamine units with one filing drawer and two storage drawers will suffice. Buy one that is on castors, so it will slide under a desk. Some computer desk units have a pull-out keyboard shelf and extra drawers and shelves for computer accessories and manuals.

Stationery This can easily get out of control, so if your present cupboard is inadequate, invest in furniture to contain it, such as a tall metal unit with three shelves and lockable doors. Smaller cupboards with one shelf are also available. A slimline multi-drawer cabinet can adequately hold business stationery. Compartmentalized insert trays can be added for loose items such as paperclips, pens and markers. For home use, stylish plastic pull-out drawer units on castors will absorb miscellaneous piece of stationery. Slimline stacking boxes in transparent plastic look good sitting on shelves, and will hold disks, CD Rom disks and index cards.

If you are on a tight budget, these inexpensive cardboard boxes will hold different items.

Printer paper Rather than leaving packs of paper lying on the floor, improve matters with a cabinet where the printer sits on top and paper is stored on shelves in the cupboard below.

Catalogues, brochures and reports

These are very messy when scattered around an office, so file in box files and label clearly. Store these on open metal or wooden shelving units, bringing the files to the edge to stop the sharp edges creating cutting chi. Or they can be secreted in stackable modular units with pull-down doors. In the home office, transparent plastic lidded stacking boxes or plastic magazine holders will keep brochures or catalogues stored neatly.

Reference books Stand in rows on open metal or wood shelving units as above, but never position a unit behind a desk because it can send out cutting chi. Ideally, look for a unit with deep shelves fitted with doors to counteract this problem, or use freestanding cabinets with several shelves and glass or wooden doors.

Where Memories Live on

All too often, the loft or attic becomes a memorial junkyard to our past. We seem to feel that this space above us can symbolically oppress us with our past emotions – our elation at success in school or sport, our sadness at the loss of relatives or failure in various projects. It encompasses the pain and passion of love affairs, the pride and unconditional love of parenthood. The past spirit of the home seems to rest here, lingering over the family like a murky cloud. The loft can also be a repository for feelings of disapproval and dislike, as we secrete more and more unwanted gifts in this deep, dark space.

The flow of energy through this higher storage area is naturally sluggish as there tends to be little ventilation. However, it is important that chi is able to move – if the loft is full to the brim with junk, it will struggle to move at all, and become an inhibiting heaviness that looms over the house.

If your room is like this, consider why you feel you need to hold on to so many reminders of your past – are you worried or frightened about what the future might hold?

THE ENERGY TRAPS

Inevitably, the loft is the area that holds many different possessions, but it is what is placed here and how it is stored that really matters.

ENERGY GRIDLOCK

Chi flows up to the chaotic loft and is immediately stopped by piles of boxes. It struggles sluggishly over scattered sports equipment, boxes of old toys, boxed games, decaying picture frames, clothes and other junk before going out the trap door.

KEY: A chi enters; B boxes of junk and mementoes; C school memorabilia; D Christmas decorations; E old sports gear; F toy boxes; G boxed games; H clothes; I chi leaves

ENERGY FREEWAY

Chi travels into the overhauled loft, moving freely around storage boxes, a boot rack, other boxed items, sporting equipment, rarely used jackets, DIY equipment, stored games and sports gear to leave by the trap door.

KEY: A chi enters; B mementoes box; C ordered boot rack; D labelled storage boxes; E ski bag; F rack with outdoor jackets; G DIY unit; H storage rack for games and sports items; I chi leaves

Overloading your loft with too much junk can symbolically restrict your higher achievements and aims, and create a fear of what the future may bring.

Empty boxes It always seems a good idea to keep these in case they come in useful for something. However, they waste space and give out stagnant energy. Select several sturdy boxes for emergencies, remove any staples carefully and fold them flat.

School memorabilia Boxes of old exercise books and awards drag you down. Even if you are proud of your achievements, they are still linking you inexorably with your past.

Boxes of romantic mementoes Ageing, dusty love letters tied in ribbon along with other special mementoes from past relationships tend to give off a musty, sad energy that can be difficult to shift.

Board games and cards Stacks of old games and cards, once played every Christmas and holiday, but now hardly used, create dull, stuck energy.

Old appliances and sports and fitness equipment Cumbersome, rusting equipment takes up space and will probably never be used again. Its bulky presence causes irritation and annoyance.

Family memorabilia Boxes containing reminders of everything that your children ever achieved at school or university again pull you back to the past, restricting new, exciting growth ahead.

Boxes of miscellaneous items A dumping ground for unwanted or discarded items that you never got around to sorting out, this cache of unresolved mess can make you feel stuck and may cause depression.

A refuge for the past

Clearing out this room is an arduous task, so before you start, assess the extent of the problem (see checklist). If it is dull and musty and so crowded with articles associated with your past life that you cannot move around easily, you must loosen your grip on the past.

PRESSURE FROM ABOVE

New experiences won't be able to come into your life until you let go of the old ones symbolized by all the outgrown possessions and mementoes stored here. If you have spent most of your life collecting and storing artefacts

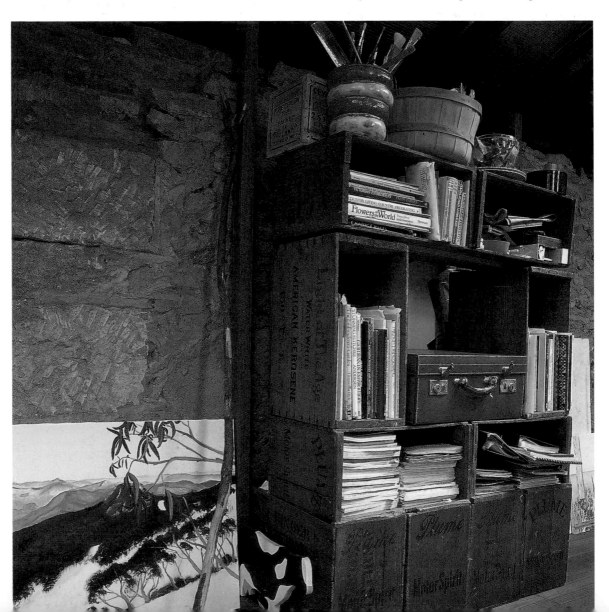

and little-used possessions, it may be a sign that you did not relish your life at that time. By tying yourself to the unwanted and unused, you have allowed sentiment to restrict you like a ball and chain. Sloping ceilings will add to the feeling of pressure and being compressed that the loft creates for members of the household.

COLOUR, MOOD AND LIGHTING

The energy in a loft is very yin and passive and will have a natural tendency to stagnate because normally there are no windows – no outlets – for it to escape through. Light creams, yellows or pastel shades of paint will help to make the room brighter and more appealing. Although it is not worth spending a lot on lighting, putting in some spotlights or bulkhead lighting will help to lift the dull energy.

All too often, our past life seems to be stored in the loft (far left) and we hang on to too many sentimental papers (left). Be ruthless and keep only what you really want on efficient shelving units such as these (above).

Re-designed space

You may feel exhausted after clearing out the loft, because it contained so many extraneous items from the past, but you now need storage systems for everything that qualifies living there. Plan carefully, as this area can easily become cluttered again, slowing down energy that already struggles to flow freely. Put the items you need to access most frequently near the loft hatch. Create organized space with planned shelving units and durable storage boxes, and you will allow calming energy to float down into the rest of the house.

Basic shelving units are easy to buy and can take care of bulky ski boots or walking shoes. Skis can be stored next to them or in protective ski bags.

LOFT CLUTTER CHECKLIST

Search through all the junk from your past, sorting it into different piles for the five-bag system (see page 31).

◆ Boxes: these seem so useful but just sit there collecting dust, so throw them out. Keep appliance boxes for the guarantee period and then get rid of them.

◆ Schoolbooks, clothes, diplomas, medals, sashes: you know your achievements, so dump these links to your youth.

◆ Love letters, dried flowers, old cards: if you can't bear to part with all of them, keep a few really special items and bin the rest.

◆ Games and cards: keep the ones that are still used, and give the rest to a hospital or a children's home.

◆ Old equipment such as exercise bikes, hockey sticks and footballs: admit to yourself that these will never be used again, and throw out or donate to sports clubs.

◆ Christmas and other holiday decorations: discard damaged items and tatty pieces of tinsel.

STORAGE SOLUTIONS

Games and card sets

Stack favourites neatly on shelving units, putting card packs in small cardboard boxes. If there is enough height for freestanding wooden or metal units with wide shelves, these will accommodate a lot of items, otherwise single melamine

Hardwearing boxes on wheels are ideal for the loft as they can be easily moved around.

or wooden shelves on metal struts are a good budget solution.

Love memorabilia Choose a special wicker, rattan, natural fibre or leather box for these precious mementoes, so that it emphasizes the love that you still feel for them. Put it somewhere that is easy to reach, so if you are in a sentimental mood you can get it down to have another look at your treasures.

Ski clothes, sports clothes and hiking or walking jackets

Put in plastic garment bags to protect them from dirt and dust and hang on clothing rails or store tidily in large, labelled plastic boxes.

Walking or hiking boots

Clean well and store on sturdy shoe racks or in large hanging

Place your love letters in an appealing box that you will cherish.

units suspended from a hook in the wall.

Decorations, gardening and DIY equipment and miscellaneous items

Place these in solid plastic or substantial cardboard stacking boxes with lids and label the contents of each box clearly. Store them in relevant groups, stacked one on top of each other, taking care to make them accessible. Tiny accessories, screws, nails or other small DIY items can be put into different-sized chest units, with small, labelled pull-out drawers, made from plywood or a similar inexpensive wood.

Clutter on the Move

A car can be very much an extension of our personalities – a mobile possession that projects another part of us. So much time is spent in our cars travelling to and from destinations that we form a strong, almost emotional, attachment to it. We choose it partly because of the appeal of its colour, style, design and look. It is our own private little world, where we want to feel safe and secure.

While driving, it is obviously important to stay bright and alert, so the chi in the car needs to be positive and very yang. If your car is a rubbish bin on wheels, the chi will find it difficult to flow around strongly. This can have a profound effect on you, slowing your reactions and decision-making skills and causing you to drive in a less assured or coordinated way.

THE ENERGY TRAPS

Hoarding things in your car will affect you as much as amassing junk in your home, because you are recreating this disturbed energy on the move. A good clear-out will bring about a major energy shift.

In the boot This area can become a black hole where piles of articles such as shoes, jackets or sports items are all dumped. This will only become a bootful of heavy energy, which may disturb your concentration as you are driving around.

ENERGY GRIDLOCK

Chi flows into the junk-filled car and is obstructed by parking tickets, receipts and discarded CDs. It tries to move over thrown food packaging, toys and atlases before exiting. In the boot, chi has problems working around a scrunched up rug, jackets, sports shoes and car accessories before leaving.

KEY: A chi enters; B parking tickets, receipts and other paper; C piles of CDs; D food and drink cartons; E dumped atlases; F abandoned toys; G chi leaves; H chi enters boot; I messy rug; J piles of jackets; K training shoes; L car accessories; M chi leaves

Door pockets and compartments Can you never find the map or atlas you want because there is so much crammed in these storage sections? This sort of clutter can cloud your thinking, making you feel confused.

Seats Are you embarrassed to offer a friend a lift because there is hardly any space for her to sit down? Are CDs, cassette tapes, empty bottles and parking tickets scattered over seats and floor? Can you never get the seats forward to let people in, because of junk stuffed behind them? This type of disorder may well reflect how you organize your life.

A car is an important possession for most of us, and, like our homes, needs to be regularly assessed for clutter because this slows the chi movement inside it which can adversely affect our driving skills.

ENERGY FREEWAY

Chi moves into the spruced up car, proceeds evenly around the CD box and cleared floor into the back over cleaned seats, stored road books and rubbish bin and out of the window. Chi comes into the boot and circulates well around the storage box and car rug before leaving.

KEY: A chi enters; B CD storage box; C cleaned seats; D atlas storage case; E hanging rubbish bin; F chi leaves; G chi enters boot; H car accessory box; I neatly rolled rug; J chi leaves

A world on the move

Sorting out your car's junk will be a huge relief, but before you get started (see checklist), stand back and look at your car. Do you feel pride when you look at it? Or do you feel ashamed because it is so dirty and shabby? Remember that in feng shui, it is believed that what is going on in our outer life is reflected inside us.

COLOUR AND ATMOSPHERE

Colour has a strong influence on us, so the colour of your car will affect how you behave when you're on the road. In feng shui terms, red is yang and therefore very stimulating,

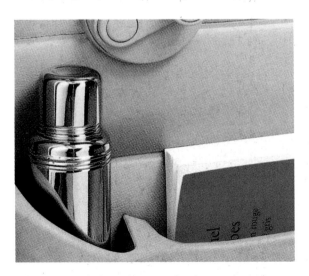

Tidy away regularly used items in the door pockets of your car, rather than leaving them on the seats.

sometimes causing anger and irritability, so this may well make you drive faster or rather aggressively. Yellow is uplifting and encourages an optimistic attitude while driving. Blue and green are calming, as they are more yin (passive) colours, and will create a relaxed atmosphere for driving. Black or grey are very yin; black will give comfort and protection in a car, while grey encourages self-reliance. White and silver are very yang colours – white gives protection, while silver promotes harmony and balance when travelling.

Dust and dirt will taint the atmosphere inside a car, so clean it out regularly. Interior surfaces are often plastic and therefore yang. If they are grey, they will shield you from outside influences. Fabric and leather seats are yin, and their softness counteracts the hard yang lines of the plastic. As always, good feng shui requires a balance of yin and yang energies, so there needs to be an equal presence of these two in your car.

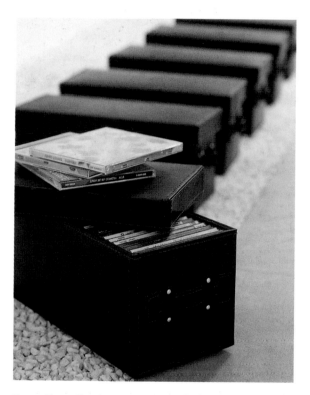

Keep all your favourite music for the car in a handy CD box.

STORAGE SOLUTIONS

Road maps and atlases Keep these in the door pockets rather than on or under the seat, or if you have a lot of them, store them together in a clean plastic briefcase, and place this tidily behind a seat.

CDs, cassette tapes and books Place these in plastic storage boxes or padded zipped cases which can be stored in the glove compartment or on the back seat.

Litter If you really can't keep this under control, place a small plastic rubbish bin in the car and empty it regularly. Some styles hook on to the car doors.

Miscellaneous car items Put car oil, jump leads, the tyre pump and other useful car accessories into a sturdy plastic storage box. Make sure it is an adequate size for your needs and comes with a lid so that items don't rattle around loose in the boot.

CAR CLUTTER CHECKLIST

If your car is a mess, get some bin liners to remove the rubbish.

◆ Road maps, atlases: search through these carefully, discard out-of-date versions and give away maps that are no longer needed.

◆ Food wrappers, cartons, empty bottles, parking tickets: search out and destroy all this stagnant energy.

◆ CDs, cassette tapes and story tapes: keep a select few of your favourites, change these regularly to create new energy, and take the rest back into the house.

◆ Shoes, coats, sports gear, miscellaneous car items: these are generating stale energy, so remove them and store indoors.

The Walking Clutter Mountain

If clutter has invaded your home and car, it is likely that this disorganization has spread to the possessions that you carry around with you.

HANDBAGS

These are very personal items, chosen with care. They show an aspect of our personalities, and are linked to the overall style that we like to present to friends and colleagues. So why do so many of us fill them up with useless articles?

If you are trying to portray a positive, confident, organized attitude, owning a bulging, over-loaded handbag reveals that there are areas of disorder in your life.

Contents overload

Scribbled notes and phone numbers, old shopping lists, vouchers, receipts, restaurant bills, numerous pens that don't work, several hairbrushes and old make-up – all slow you down by creating pools of dull energy.

Solutions Sort through your bag, throwing away useless papers and pens, and transfer phone numbers to your address book or Filofax. Dispense with old make-up, keep current items in a neat make-up bag and retain one hairbrush. Remove receipts and vouchers and file in a plastic folder with sections – review regularly and discard them when no longer needed.

Rather than keeping new phone numbers on scraps of paper transfer them to your Filofax or personal organizer.

PURSES AND WALLETS

Overcrowding these with extraneous matter can have a negative effect on your current finances.

Contents overload Old business cards, out-of-date credit cards, membership cards, appointment cards and credit card vouchers can all drain your finances.

Solutions Take out the business cards and record useful numbers and addresses in your address book, write appointments in your diary and cut up expired credit and membership cards. File credit card vouchers in a folder and review monthly to keep in order.

BRIEFCASES

Like handbags, briefcases reflect some of your character, and contribute to the impression you

give to colleagues and clients. Even if you are dressed smartly, a crammed, shabby briefcase will indicate disorganization and lack of control.

Contents overload Old files, memos, unread reports, unanswered correspondence, broken pens and pencils, reference books – all slow you down and bring in chaos.

An ordered briefcase will help you stay in control of your working life (above).
Keep paper to the minimum by transferring addresses to your address book and appointments to your diary (left).

Solutions Note the contents of memos and throw them away. Remove files that you don't need and put them back in the office. Create an office action folder for correspondence. Read reports and return them to the office. Throw out old stationery and keep a couple of working pens and pencils in a pocket in your briefcase. Return reference books to their sources. Resolve from now on to carry only the paperwork that you need for meetings or working at home.

Energize with Feng Shui Cures

It's taken time, but you've finally got to grips with your clutter and worked through the emotional loss of throwing away belongings that you have become attached to over the years. You've done a space-clearing ceremony to release any trapped negative energies clinging to your home, but what next? Perhaps the atmosphere around you still feels a bit dull and in need of a lift. For a thorough feng shui analysis, you need the services of a consultant, who can harmonize the home's energies and the surrounding environment. But there are some simple feng shui enhancements and cures that you can apply yourself to raise your home's energy vibrations and make it a brighter, more appealing place to live.

HOW DO THEY WORK?

Enhancements boost the energy around the eight life aspiration areas of the Pa Kua (see pages 14–15) such as your relationship or wealth corner. Cures can be carefully positioned to offset any problems or correct negative energy affecting the room's

Candlelight is always inspiring and brings in positive yang energy to a room.

WHAT CAN YOU USE?

There are several different types of feng shui cure and enhancement that can be placed around your home:

• Mirrors lift energy and expand spaces, but need to be used with caution in the bedroom.

• The soft, tinkly sound of wind chimes is either used to slow down the flow of chi or encourage its circulation in the home.

• Crystals have a strong vibrational energy and their uses include activating the career area, healing, and attracting more energy into a room.

• Water features or aquariums encourage money to flow into your life when placed in your wealth area.

• Lights or candles bring strong yang energy to stagnant areas, or can raise the energy in your fame section.

• Plants are versatile feng shui cures. Their healthy, positive energy can help alleviate problem areas.

• Attaching bamboo flutes to overhead beams helps to reduce the negative impact.

• Metal and electrical items enhance the energy of the west.

• Paired items represent togetherness and romance and can strengthen an existing relationship or entice new partners into your life.

• Mirrors shaped like the Pa Kua, situated only outside the home near the front door, help to deflect any bad energy attacking the home.

atmosphere. For example, healthy plants are positive and yang, and can be used to shield people against harmful cutting chi emanating from a corner or pillar. Plants can also lessen the effects of electromagnetic stress that comes from a television or other electrical equipment.

By harmonizing the energies in each room, you will feel your home start to come alive again and work positively for you.

MIRRORS

In the past, mirrors were considered so special that only people such as pharaohs, kings and shamans were allowed to use them. In feng shui, mirrors are powerful tools. A flat mirror expands energy, and will open up a narrow space such as a hallway, lightening the area and creating the illusion of more space.

Symbolically, a mirror can also 'double' energy. So if it is placed opposite a dining table, for example, it 'doubles' the value of the food on the table, and is believed to increase the family's wealth. However, don't be tempted to put a mirror opposite your cluttered desk, because it will double your existing workload.

Mirrors also serve the symbolic purpose of making things 'disappear'. So if your toilet faces the front door, which according to feng shui is a very bad position, putting a mirror on the toilet door will in effect make it 'disappear'. Another function of mirrors is dealing with irregularly shaped rooms, which are believed to be inauspicious as they will have a section of the Pa Kua missing. A 'missing corner' can be reinstated by using a mirror. For example, if your home has a missing corner in the career

A mirror is very yang, so in a bathroom can help to lift the slow energy that exists there.

area, placing a mirror facing inwards on one wall of the L-shape will symbolically restore it.

It is possible to buy eight-sided mirrors shaped like the Pa Kua. These are very powerful, so use them carefully. Never place a pa kua mirror inside the home, but it can be hung outside your front door to fend off bad energies such as the cutting chi coming from a road directly opposite. But position it with care, making sure that it does not reflect neighbouring homes and send bad energy to them.

Mirror lore

• Never position mirrors facing each other, because they will bounce chi back and forth.

• Don't use a cracked or tarnished mirror as it literally and symbolically distorts your image.

• Keep mirrors sparkling clean. When not in use, store face down, otherwise they can bring confusion into your life.

• Do not hang a mirror to reflect your bed, because its energy can cause restlessness and insomnia.

• Never place a mirror opposite your front door, because it will send the good energy that enters out again.

A metal wind chime can lift the chi in the west of a room.

WIND CHIMES

In ancient China, wind chimes were traditionally hung to frighten away unsettled spirits. But nowadays in modern feng shui they have a more positive influence in the home. When a wind chime is positioned inside a front door that opens opposite a staircase, for example, incoming chi that would otherwise rush straight up the stairs is filtered and slowed down by the beautiful tinkling chimes. Hung inside or outside, wind chimes ward off negative forces, activate chi, and raise chi in a dull area.

Suspended outside the front door, a melodious five-rod metal wind chime can deflect cutting chi coming off the corners of other buildings.

When choosing a wind chime to lift energy in a room, first find out the room's direction and element so that you know whether to hang metal, ceramic or wooden wind chimes. In the west (Metal), northwest (Metal) and north (Water is produced by Metal), metal wind chimes are best. Ceramic chimes will suit the southwest (Earth) and northeast (Earth). Wooden chimes work well in the east (Wood), southeast (Wood) and south (the Fire element is produced by Wood).

CRYSTALS

A small, sparkling, lead-faceted crystal sphere dangling in a sunny window spreads an inspiring rainbow of beautiful colours across the walls. Everyone will notice its uplifting effect as it raises the energy vibrations of the room. If you position it in a specific area of the Pa Kua, it will bring extra energy to that sector. In your wealth area, for example, you will notice that your bank balance stays healthy and that money seems to come your way more easily.

Crystals are good for energizing areas of your home. Natural quartz (see opposite) can boost your relationship corner in the southwest of your living room.

Hang or place a crystal in a room, after clutter has been cleared out, to create a significant shift in energy flow. Crystals also reduce negativity, deflecting cutting chi aimed at the house by telegraph poles or bus stops. A 20mm sphere is the right size for activating a small room, while a 30mm crystal is better for an average room. Hang the crystal from a drawing pin near the top of the window in the centre of a pane.

If you are seeking a new relationship, or if an existing one needs some help, a powerful natural quartz cluster can energize the southwest (relationship) corner of your lounge, while an amethyst crystal will stimulate the northeast (education and knowledge) sector.

Rose quartz is associated with romance, so again place in the southwest. Its soothing qualities will also calm disruptive children, if it is placed in their bedroom.

Crystal tips

• Cleanse new crystals briefly under cold water. If they were bought in a big crystal shop, soak for 24 hours to remove other energies.

• Clean hanging crystals weekly by dipping in still spring mineral water and leaving to dry.

• To activate the powers of a crystal, mentally state your intention for it when you hang it up.

• Amethyst is a wonderful healing stone. Use it to aid recovery from illness.

WATER FEATURES

The trickling sound of flowing water is soothing. Water is a wonderful carrier of chi, and it can entice positive energy into your home. Water is also traditionally associated with wealth by the Chinese.

The best place for an indoor water feature is the southeast (Wood and wealth) corner of your home or your lounge. This is because in the cycle of the five elements, Water produces Wood.

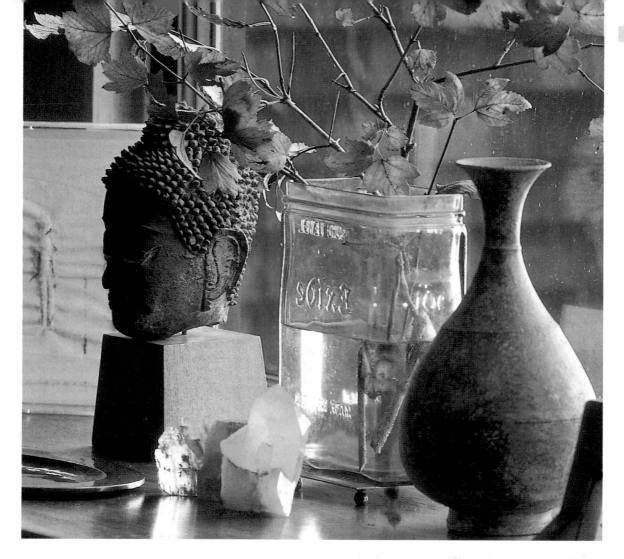

Choose a small indoor fountain, a trickling water feature or an aquarium. It is preferable to have an odd number of fish in an aquarium, with nine considered to be very lucky. Ideally, one should be a different colour to absorb negative energy, so eight orange goldfish and one black one would be a good combination. The constant motion of the oxygenated water and the fish stimulate the chi in the water. A pond or a small fountain on the left-hand side of your front garden encourages the flow of good energy to your home. Fountains also deflect any cutting chi that is adversely affecting your home. Always keep water clean and fresh to avoid the pitfalls of stagnancy.

Do not put a water feature or image of water in your bedroom, because Water overwhelms Earth in the element cycle (and the bedroom is considered to be Earth). A surfeit of Water is thought to cause relationship problems.

LIGHTING

Lights can bathe a room in soft, warm light, provide localized light for reading, or dramatically light a dinner table. They affect our moods, stimulating or relaxing us. Contemporary lighting is an integral part of interior design and also plays an important part in feng shui. Lights link to the Fire element, bringing positive yang energy to every room. They encourage the flow of chi, particularly in the south. Carefully planned lighting creates balance and harmony.

Where possible, choose table and floor lamps that relate to the element of the areas where they are being placed. For example, rounded, oval or dome shapes work best in the west and northwest, which link to Metal. Tall, straight lights are appropriate for the east and southeast sections that relate to Wood. Flowing, wavy or irregular shapes are associated with Water and will enhance areas in the north.

Soft candlelight can promote a relaxing ambience in a room.

CANDLES

Soft, flickering candles bring a natural light and yang energy, and add a special atmosphere to a living or dining room. In the bedroom, candles give off a soft light, creating a gentle aura of romance.

Bathrooms are usually steamy and humid, therefore the energy here will be very slow-moving. Plain or scented candles situated by the bath tub or in wall sconces lift this energy while imbuing the area with a warm, ambient glow – ideal for a room where we need to feel completely relaxed.

PLANTS

Healthy green plants are living feng shui enhancements that give out oxygen, generating a special chi that engenders a fresher, lively atmosphere. As energizers, they lift stagnant energy in dark corners, and when sited near electrical equipment they counterbalance negative electromagnetic fields. They have the ability to remove toxins from the air, can obscure cutting chi from sharp-angled furniture or columns, and can slow down chi that moves too fast down a long corridor.

However, the shape of a plant's leaves is important. Spiky-leaved plants are believed to send out bad chi from their sharp leaves, so choose varieties with rounded, succulent leaves to attract auspicious chi.

Burning candles in the bedroom brings a romantic feel to this tranquil room.

In the bathroom, plants absorb humidity and raise chi levels, while in a kitchen they can increase the existing yang energy. However, do not place them near the cooker, because their Wood element will fuel the Fire energy of the cooker too much.

In order to enhance and strengthen the Wood element in your home, you can site plants in the east (associated with family and health) and the southeast (lilnked with wealth and prosperity). A money plant in your wealth area is believed to mirror your fortunes according to how well it grows. Plants can also boost corners in the south of your home (representing Fire, fame and recognition), because Wood feeds Fire in the cycle of elements.

Index

Acknowledgements

I would like to thank Cindy Richards for giving me the opportunity to write this book, and Liz Dean for all her hard work in putting it together. Also Roger Daniels for his great design, and Sam Wilson for her witty illustrations and Kate Simunek for her patience in doing some difficult artworks. My appreciation also goes to my feng shui master Harrison Kyng for setting me off on the wonderful path of feng shui. Finally, thanks to my family and all my friends for their encouragement during the difficult stages of writing, and my boyfriend Steve for his constant support and invaluable advice on clutter in the car.

FURTHER READING

Clear Your Clutter with feng shui, Karen Kingston, Piatkus
Creating Sacred Space with feng shui, Karen Kingston, Piatkus
Sacred Space, Denise Linn, Rider Books
Clear Your Desk! Declan Treacy, Arrow Business Books
Ligten Up! Free Yourself from Clutter, Michelle Passoff, Harper Perennial
Home Design From the Inside Out, Robin Lennon with Karen Plunkett-Powell, Penguin Arkana
Clutter's Last Stand, Don Aslett, Writer's Digest Books
Feng shui for Modern Living, Stephen Skinner and Mary Lambert, Cima Books

Mary Lambert is based in London and can be contacted for feng shui consultations on homes and businesses and for clutter clearing sessions on 0800 975 6021

PICTURE CREDITS

The publishers are grateful to the following for permission to reproduce photographs:
Abode UK: pages 39 above and below, 41,43; Tim Beddow/Interior Archive: page 44; Simon Brown/Interior Archive: pages 19, 40 above, 42 right; Josie Clyde/Stock Shot: page 78; The Cotswold Company: pages 37 above, 42 left, 58, 59 centre, 62, 69, 70, 79 below; Crabtree & Evelyn: page 20; Michael Crockett/Elizabeth Whiting Associates: page 16; Michael Dunne/Elizabeth Whiting Associates: page 51; Laurence Dutton/The General Trading Company: page 53; Feng Shui for Modern Living/Centennial Publishing: pages 30, 52, 86, 89; Filofax: page 85 below left; GettyOne Stone: pages 15, 25, 83 above right; David Giles/Elizabeth Whiting Associates: page 88; The Holding Company: pages 9, 37 below right, 40 below, 59 left, 68, 72 left and right, 83; Jacqui Hurst: page 23 above and below; Rodney Hyett/Elizabeth Whiting Associates: pages 57 and 76; Tom Leighton/Elizabeth Whiting Associates: page 49; Nadia Mackenzie/Interior Archive: page 46; Muji: pages 71, 73, 77, 79 above; Neo Vision/Photonica: pages 11, 21, 66, 87; Michael Nicholson/Elizabeth Whiting Associates: page 91; Osprey by Graeme Ellisdon: page 84; Peugeot: page 82; Pictor International: page 81; The Pier: pages 32, 35, 59 right, 63, 92, 93; T. Sawada/Photonica: page 90; Fritz von der Schulenburg/ Interior Archive: pages 34, 54, 65; Karin Taylor/ Marie Claire/IPC Syndication: page 27; Pia Tryde/The General Trading Company: page 13 above; The White Company: page 64 above and below; Elizabeth Whiting Associates; page 48; Henry Wilson/Interior Archive: page 13 below, 56, 60.

Picture research by Gabrielle Allen